What Others Are Saying about
The Invisible Path to Success:

"I've done personal growth trainings for ten years. I've noticed patterns in the problems people come in wanting to solve, and the goals they want to achieve. It's changing so dramatically, frankly, it was getting to the point where I didn't always know how to help my clients, and sometimes even myself, until I discovered *The Invisible Path to Success*."

— **Nick Daley, Dallas, Texas**
Formerly a top trainer with Tony Robbins

"I now consider myself 100% cured of CFIDS (Chronic Fatigue Immune Dysfunction Syndrome), which most mainstream medical practitioners say can't happen. People at work started noticing I had more energy and I looked much better. I have so much more confidence knowing that whatever comes up in my life I can deal with it instead of running away and trying to ignore it."

— **Lance Allen, Artesia, New Mexico**

"I've purchased hundreds of books, tapes, videocassettes and even a brain wave machine. Nothing worked when things got really bad until I got your system. It has given me the tools to not only make it through tough times, but prevent the pain from happening in the first place. I don't feel like a ping-pong ball just bouncing around anymore. For the first time I feel part of the system, not a pawn."

— **Mike Hendricks, Houston, Texas**

"*The Invisible Path to Success* created a safe place for me to make major identity and behavior changes. Using your system, I've experienced clarity in finding out what I really want. Fear, uncertainty, and doubt have been replaced with excitement, action, and positive outcomes. I'm a more alive, joyous person. I feel more now—and I think less."

— **Jim Brown, Mesa, Arizona**

"I know myself now in a totally different way. I'm achieving things in my life I never knew possible. It's truly outstanding."

— **Tom Lloyd, Los Angeles, Talent Agent**

"For the first time in months, I really feel I have some type of handle on my next step. I've been almost immobilized by indecision, pain, hurt, etc. You've given me back my faith in myself and the Universe."

— *Chris Bice, Laramie, Wyoming,*
Financial Planner

"I do congratulate you on being 'to the point' and specific. I found so many other courses to be long on theory and short on practicality."

— *John Economides, Elmwood Park, New Jersey*

"The material is real and has staying power. It has every day, over-and-over usability. I've been to so many seminars in my adult life and most have helped me but left me feeling they weren't complete. *They weren't!* Now I have what I need to do the job. I won't ever again go to the 'toolbox' and find I need something that isn't there."

— *Lee Johnson, Greeley, Colorado,*
Insurance Broker

"I thought your system was going to be like any other program or book, with techniques and ways to do things which don't work but, instead, make you more hopeless and depressed. After using your system I now have the confidence I needed *urgently.* I also am more at peace with myself and have a slower paced, gentler life. Thank you, Bob, for making my dreams come true."

—*Mohhanad Hassouneh, Ontario, Canada*

"I can't even begin to tell you the impact your system has had on me. It's the most incredible thing I've come across in a long time."

— *Richard Lim, Toronto, Canada,*
Newsletter Publisher

"To have something be so mind blowing and yet so common sense was incredible! I'm walking away with a sense of calm and peacefulness I never felt before."

— *Jeff Coulter, Colorado Springs, Colorado*
Training Manager

THE INVISIBLE PATH TO

SUCCESS

ROBERT SCHEINFELD

Seven Steps to Understanding and Managing
The Unseen Forces Shaping Your Life

HAMPTON ROADS
PUBLISHING COMPANY, INC.

For information write:

Hampton Roads Publishing Company, Inc.
134 Burgess Lane
Charlottesville, VA 22902

Or call: (804) 296-2772
FAX: (804) 296-5096
e-mail: hrpc@hrpub.com
Website: www.hrpub.com

Library of Congress Catalog Card Number: 98-071239

ISBN 1-57174-083-X

If you are unable to order this book from your local
bookseller, you may order directly from the publisher.
Quantity discounts for organizations are available.
Call 1-800-766-8009, toll-free.

10 9 8 7 6 5 4 3 2 1

Printed on acid-free paper in the United States of America

To everyone who chooses
to consciously navigate
"The Invisible Path to Success"

Acknowledgments

This book is the result of an extraordinary and very painful journey I took during my mid-to-late thirties.

Without the support, love, and help I received from Ava Brenner and her "guys," Les Ferry and Susan Jean, I don't know if I would have survived that journey or come out of it with the clarity it took to write this book. From the bottom of my heart, I thank you all and say that I will be eternally grateful for the tremendous gifts you gave me when I needed them most.

Special thanks must also go to my parents, Jim and Audrey, for agreeing to bring me into this world and for setting into motion the many forces that shaped who I've become in this lifetime.

I'd also like to thank Frank DeMarco and Bob Friedman for believing in me when so few others did, and my editor, Sharon Goldinger, for helping me sculpt my "piece of clay" into this book.

To my beloved and beautiful wife, Cecily, thank you so very much for finding your way into my life and for shining such a sweet, warm, and bright light where there was so much numbness, coldness, and darkness. I love you more than I can ever express in words and I cherish every moment we have together.

Introduction

Success. Since you're reading this book, you must want it in your life.

But what is success? What is it *really?* On the surface, it's not an easy question to answer.

We've all been so programmed, conditioned, media-blitzed, and pressured into looking at success in certain ways, and it seems we rarely take the time to ask what success really means to us—as unique human beings.

I'm going to be sharing some very unusual definitions of success in this book—and some very unusual pathways to achieve it. I call these definitions and pathways "The Invisible Path to Success."

There are seven steps you must take before you can see this path clearly enough to navigate it. This book will introduce you to those seven steps and give you specific instructions for navigating the path anywhere you *really* want to go.

Every day you have thoughts. You have feelings. Things happen to you. How much is caused by you and how much by someone else? How much is fate, destiny, or the result of invisible forces you know nothing about?

Who are you—really? Why are you here on Earth? Is there a purpose for your life, for the lives of everyone else you see—or is everyone and everything the result of accident and chance?

These are important questions. No matter what you want in life, from the smallest goal to the most grand or dramatic dream, you must have practical and usable answers to these questions. Otherwise, it's like trying to get around a strange city without directions or a map.

So many times we look to what we call the "surface world," the "visible world," or the "physical world" for answers to these questions. But we don't find them. We don't find them because they're not there. The answers to these questions are beneath the surface; they're behind the scenes; they're invisible to the naked eye.

Our libraries, bookstores, mail-order catalogs, the Internet, and the speeches of our public speakers and trainers are filled with suggestions, formulas, and techniques you can use to change your life, get more of what you want, and become more successful.

If you take all the really good success and personal development approaches (even the more mystical or metaphysical ones) and boil their messages down, they all pretty much say the same thing. "You create your own reality," they tell you. "Your thoughts, beliefs, feelings, fears, attitudes, intentions, and expectations cause everything."

In other words, your *inner* world creates your *outer* experiences. Then you're taught how to change things by using techniques like goal setting, visualization, affirmations, subliminal tapes, self-hypnosis tapes, neurolinguistic programming, meditation, prayer—the list goes on and on.

When you use these techniques, what you're really doing is asking "the Universe," or another part of yourself, to give you something you want—or change something you don't want. The interesting thing is, these techniques work for some requests but not others. They work for some people but not other people. Sometimes the changes they help you make don't last. Have you ever wondered why?

I believe we kid ourselves a lot. We want to believe in shortcuts, unlimited power, and magic so badly that we sometimes ignore the obvious things that stare us right in the face.

Think about your personal history. Do your best to add up the things you've asked for using the common suggestions, formulas, and techniques. How many of them did you actually receive?

I've been through phases in my life where I got just about everything I asked for. I've also been through phases where I didn't get a single thing I asked for.

If you look closely, I think you'll see that, in general, you receive a very small percentage of the things you *consciously* ask for in your life.

People say what you focus on you create. But take a close look again. Think about all the things you focus on every day—the things you want, the things you don't want, the things you're afraid of, the things you expect.

Do they all show up in your life? Again, if you're like me and most of the people I've worked with, you'll see that only a small percentage of what you focus on actually shows up in your life.

And when you do get what you ask for, aren't you the slightest bit curious about why or how it happened? Take visualization, affirmations, changing your beliefs, and goal setting for example. Did you ever wonder how seeing an image in your mind's eye; hearing, seeing, or repeating an affirmation over and over; changing a belief about yourself or the world; or writing goals on paper and re-reading them could actually translate into events and experiences in your daily life?

People will say your all-powerful subconscious mind does it for you, but that's not a good enough explanation. You can't consciously tap *real power* until you know the hows and whys—the "organizing principles" that make things possible.

So how do these ways of asking *(causes)* actually translate into thoughts, feelings, events, or experiences *(effects)* in your life? Why do you achieve some goals and not others? Why do techniques work sometimes and not other times; for some people and not other people? Why do some of your thoughts, beliefs, and feelings show up and others don't? Why do you get some but not all of what you focus on? In other words,

What really causes the things you think and feel and what happens to you every day?

There was a time in my life when I was curious about the answers to these questions, but I was just curious and that was it.

Then I went through a very painful seven-year period in my life where everything fell apart, where it seemed like I had the reverse of the Midas touch—where everything I touched "failed" or got incredibly messed up.

I was so confused, angry, and desperate; I had to find answers that made sense and could help me stop the pain of my downward spiral.

So I started an incredible journey. I quit my job and committed all my time, all my energy, and the rest of my money to finding answers.

After much analysis I realized that whether it's you or someone else, it's the same person asking the same way every time. So if you receive some things and not other things, if the techniques work sometimes and not other times, if the techniques work for some people but not other people, or if you get some but not all of what you focus on, then something else must be going on behind the scenes.

When you ask for something or you focus on something, there's got to be some hidden, but very powerful, force at work—some invisible force that shapes the response you get to your requests.

Through a series of amazing experiences and some very special schooling I went through, I discovered how that behind-the-scenes process works, what the invisible forces are, and how you can better manage them to receive more of what you *really* want in life. I'll be sharing what I discovered with you in this book.

I'm going to be talking here about invisible forces—unseen forces that impact your life. I'm going to be talking about things you don't normally think about or talk about. So don't be surprised if some of the things I say seem hard to believe, strange, or "far-out" at first.

Don't be surprised if you notice some conflict between what I say and what you've believed to be true for a long time. Don't be surprised if some of the things I say shock you, anger you, shake you up, or even scare you a bit. If you have such feelings, and if you want them to, they will pass over time.

You may not care, but I want you to know that even the strangest, even the most far-out things I'll be sharing with you here are now being documented by doctors and scientists all over the world.

After you take your first step you'll see that scientific proof is really not all that important, but it is readily available if you're willing to do some digging and your mind likes to have it.

Here's how the book is going to flow. As I said, there are seven steps you must take before you can start navigating The Invisible Path to Success. For each step, I'll share three things with you.

First, I'll give the step a name I hope you'll find easy to understand and remember. Then I'll explain what the step means and how it works. Then I'll give you precise, specific, detailed suggestions for using it in your life so you can get the best results and the most benefits.

The topics to be discussed here are what you might call "deep issues." I could go on about these issues for days, weeks, even years, but I have limited time here with you.

Please know that as you go through the book, if there is any step, idea, subject, or topic you want to know more about, you'll be given the opportunity. I want you to be able to travel The Invisible Path to Success as far as you want to go.

Think of this book as if it were a jigsaw puzzle. When you put together a jigsaw puzzle, you dump all the pieces on a table and at first it doesn't look like much. You start putting the pieces together and slowly but surely it starts to look like something. Finally, when all the pieces are in place, the picture explodes into view.

That's what I want to happen for you with this book. Each chapter contains a few pieces of a picture puzzle. Once you add these pieces to the pieces you've already collected in your life, a new picture of who you are, why you're here, what your purpose is, and how to better manage the unseen forces shaping your life will explode into view. Then the real fun begins.

I know you want a lot of how-to information. I know you want specifics—step-by-step plans—and I'm going to give them to you. But I've got to lay a strong foundation first.

As we go through the seven steps, I expect you'll have many insights and what I call "a-ha" experiences. But the real breakthroughs will probably come toward the end of the book, after you've taken all seven steps and the whole new picture has become very clear. Please be patient and calmly take the seven steps that make the navigating in part two possible.

A few more things before we take our first step together. I want you to know that everything I say in this book is my opinion and that's all it is. It describes life as I see it. It summarizes the conclusions I've drawn from my journeys, my experiments, my attempts to answer confusing questions and carve out a path to what I've decided success means to me.

It's awkward to always say "in my opinion" or "as I see it," so please know that it's always implied even if I don't say it or even if it sounds like I'm making a broad statement of an absolute truth that should apply to everyone.

I also want to be absolutely respectful to both men and women here, and as I'm sure you know, it can be very awkward to say "he or she" or "his or her" all the time. So, as I speak in this book, I'll say "he" and "his" sometimes and "she" and "her" sometimes. It's my intention to do this randomly and in a balanced way.

While writing this book I did my best to make things simple enough so that both adults and children could understand and benefit from it. But please don't let the simplicity fool you. Very powerful and mysterious forces are at work here. Very powerful and mysterious forces indeed!

It's my intent and sincere hope that this book will help you make changes in your life—no matter what you want or what your life is like right now.

I started *my* journey of discovering The Invisible Path to Success feeling like everyone and everything was against me, like I could do nothing right, like a cruel Universe was taking every opportunity to throw a wrench into my life or somehow mess me up—just for the twisted pleasure of seeing me squirm.

After discovering The Invisible Path to Success, the nature of my journey changed radically and I now find myself saying to my wife over and over: "I'm so excited about our life. I love what's happening!"

A dramatic turnaround, wouldn't you say? I want you to feel that excited about your life. I want you to love what's happening in your life too!

I offer this book so that it might plant seeds you'll nurture and grow on your own. I offer this book so that it might stimulate new thinking in you, new ideas in you, new possibilities for you and your life.

I offer this book so that it might help you feel stronger and more powerful, stable, confident, and competent—and less fearful, confused, vulnerable, worried, or stressed out.

In creating this book, it was my intention to open a doorway for you—a doorway that connects the visible with the invisible, the seen with the unseen, the known with the mysterious.

Albert Einstein once said:

> *The most beautiful thing we can experience is the mysterious. It is the source of all true art and all science. He to whom this emotion is a stranger, who can no longer pause to wonder and stand rapt in awe, is as good as dead. His eyes are closed.*

Having said this by way of introduction, let's open our eyes, open the doorway, walk through it, and take our first step together toward discovering The Invisible Path to Success.

Part One

*How to Discover
The Invisible Path to Success*

Chapter One

The first step toward reaching The Invisible Path to Success is what I call

*Let go of opinions
and use what works for you.*

I'm going to introduce this first step, then come back to it again in more detail after you've taken the second and third steps.

Walk into any bookstore and go into any section—you'll see lots of books on the same subject. If you were to read all those books, you'd see that while they have some things in common, most of the authors disagree on just about everything.

Assemble a group of ten experts on any topic, put them into the same room, ask them the same question, and you'll most likely hear ten different opinions.

The world has many great religions that completely disagree with each other. The disagreements are so serious sometimes that wars result.

A doctor could appear on television tomorrow morning claiming to have discovered the cure for cancer, and let's assume the doctor really found it. She could give dramatic evidence and provide extensive documentation of the validity of her discovery, and while some people would believe her and accept her discovery as true, other people would not.

A huge face could show up in the sky today claiming to be God. He could demonstrate tremendous power and offer the ultimate truth of the Universe. While some people would believe it was God and the ultimate truth, other people would deny it or think it was the devil.

When I was in a high school history class, I remember reading a thin little book called *Ten Possible Interpretations of the Cause of the American Revolution*. It had ten chapters, each written by a different author. Each author explained his or her theory of what really caused the American Revolution.

I read the first chapter and said to myself, "That makes sense. That's what really caused the revolution." But then I read the next chapter and felt the same way—even though it came to a completely different conclusion.

The same thing happened for the remaining eight chapters. They all made sense. They were all intelligent opinions. But they were totally different.

I could stand in front of you and claim I had magical powers. I could make a huge diamond or a giraffe appear out of thin air. You might believe I had magical powers. But based on some of the great magicians you've seen, like David Copperfield, or the special effects you've seen in movies, you might just think it was sleight of hand or an illusion of some kind.

Throughout history, we have absolutely believed that something was true, like when we thought the world was flat. But later, when we got more or different information, we changed our opinion. It happens in science all the time.

It has happened in your life, hasn't it? You were absolutely sure something was true until you found out it wasn't one day.

How can this be? How can so many intelligent, informed, and educated people have such different opinions and change their minds so much?

The simple answer is that life is too complicated, and even with all the brainpower and egos in the world, none of us are smart or knowledgeable enough to figure it all out. Not right now anyway.

This is especially true about the deeper, more philosophical questions such as: Who am I? Why am I here? What is my purpose? Why do things happen to me the way they do? Is there a God, and if so, what is his or her role in my life?

It doesn't matter how strongly you believe, how much proof you're given, how deeply you feel in your gut that something is true, how smart a speaker is, how many powerful demonstrations you see, or how much you trust or respect someone. You may never know what the absolute truth is about anything.

Stop and think about the significance of that for a few seconds.

For the reasons I just explained, and others that will be added later in the book, there's just no way to know what's true about anything—for sure.

How could you? How could you be *absolutely sure* about anything?

Something could make sense logically. A lot of people could agree with it. It could feel right on. But how could you ever know it was absolutely true?

I would suggest you can't. Not right now anyway.

When I came to that conclusion—that I might never know the absolute truth—you know what I decided? I decided that debates about what's true and not true, right or wrong, good or bad, correct or incorrect don't matter.

Everything is just opinion. Every opinion could be wrong. The only thing that really matters is *what works*.

If there's something you want to understand or do in your life, and you're considering ideas or someone's opinion on it, let go of what you think, let go of opinions, let go of rules, formulas, generalizations, correct, and incorrect. Experiment with an open mind and use what works for you.

Let what works for you become your standard to measure success by, not your *intellectual analysis* of what's right or wrong, good or bad, accurate or inaccurate.

Mohandas Gandhi, the famed spiritual leader from India, said:

> *[A]s long as I have not realized this absolute truth, so long must I hold by the relative truth as I have conceived it. That relative truth must, meanwhile, be my beacon, my shield and buckler. Though this path is straight and narrow, and sharp as the razor's edge, for me, it has been the quickest and easiest.*

If a particular set of beliefs, a cure for a disease, or an approach to managing finances or improving relationships works for you, and by "works" I mean it helps you produce the results you want, then it's relative truth for you, and you should continue using it as long as it continues to work for you.

But if it doesn't help you produce the results you want, discard it and keep looking until you do find something that works for you. This is the only standard to measure an idea or a belief system against. And the only way you can know if it works or not is if you have an open mind; experiment, and see for yourself.

I believe that what I'm sharing with you here is true and accurate. But whether it's true and accurate or not, it works for me so I keep using it.

It also works for people from different countries, different races, different cultures, and different backgrounds. Because it works for me and other people, it could work for you too, but the only way you'll know is if you use it and see what results you produce.

If you evaluate what you discover here in your head, just by using your intellect and analytical skills, and you accept or reject it without seeing if it works for you, you do yourself a great disservice.

It's the same with opinions you may hear about nutrition, exercise, how to run your business, how to be a better parent, how to invest your money, how to get healthy, or how to solve a problem you have. Anything!

Let go of whether you agree with it or not intellectually. Let go of whether you or someone you know thinks it's right or wrong, good or bad, accurate or inaccurate. If you feel motivated enough, and that's the key, *if you feel motivated enough,* go ahead and try it. If it works for you, use it. If it doesn't work, keep looking until you find something that does work for you.

But please, for your sake, not mine; if you're like I used to be, get out of your head and start trying things, because that's the only way you'll ever know if something is right or wrong, good or bad, accurate or inaccurate—*for you.* You can only find that out through experience—not thought.

The bottom line: If you accept that, you may never know what's true, and an effective strategy can be to experiment and use what works for you. It can help you to be more open-minded in your interactions with other people. It can also make you much more humble.

Gandhi also said:

> *The seeker after Truth should be humbler than the dust. The world crushes dust under its feet, but the seeker after*

Truth should so humble himself that even the dust could crush him. Only then, and not until then, will he have a glimpse of truth.

This step might seem simple and obvious to you, but it's the foundation upon which everything else we'll be talking about rests.

So what's the first step toward The Invisible Path to Success? Since you may never know the absolute truth,

**Let go of opinions and
use what works for you!**

Chapter Two

The second step is what I call

Take your seats to the best show in town.

I'm going to spend a lot of time on this step before moving on, because it's the absolute key to discovering and navigating The Invisible Path to Success.

Do you like movies? I'm going to assume you answered yes because so many of the people I talk to like them. If for some reason you don't like movies, follow along anyway. You'll still see the point I'm trying to make.

So you like movies. Why? Think about it.

When I talk to people from all over the world, they tell me there are four main reasons they like movies:

1. They're fun.
2. They provide an escape from your daily routine.
3. You learn and grow from them.
4. You experience different points of view and have different experiences.

If you come up with another reason, let me know and I'll add it to the list.

Interestingly, a movie is not what I call a "total immersion" experience. No matter how good it is, no matter how involved you are, you know you're in the theater; you're aware of your chair, the other people, and the screen. What is most important, while you get a glimpse, you don't know what the people up on the screen are really thinking or feeling. There's a distance, a barrier between you and them—a barrier between you and *their* experience.

What if I told you I could take you to a very special movie theater where you'd temporarily forget who you were and totally immerse yourself in any character, story, subject, or experience that interested you. You could actually become the other characters for a while—think what they think, know what they know, do what they do, experience what they experience—then come back out of the movie and be yourself again, but be incredibly changed and enriched by the experience.

I'm talking about going way beyond what's now being called virtual reality. I'm talking about totally immersing yourself in any adventure, any character, or any kind of experience that interests you.

You could be the president of the United States, the Super Bowl-winning quarterback, a gold medal-winning athlete, a billionaire, a spy behind enemy lines, a musician, a serial killer, a parent of twins, a general leading an army into battle, a spiritual leader, a researcher trying to solve our pollution problems—anything that interests you. Anything!

It doesn't need to be grand or dramatic either. It can be simple and low-key too. There are no judgments here. It's just about what interests you.

You'd actually become one of these characters—temporarily—and think everything he thinks, feel everything he feels, say everything he says, be everything he is, and do everything he does. You'd be totally safe and protected so no harm could come to you.

26

Would you want to go to a movie theater like that? Would you want to experience a total immersion movie adventure like that?

Again, I'm going to assume you said yes because just about everybody I talk to would love to—as long as they knew they'd be absolutely safe.

If for some reason you wouldn't like to have an experience like that, please continue reading. You'll find tremendous benefit from this line of thinking anyway.

Earth represents the same experience. Think of it as a very special kind of amusement park where three-dimensional, total immersion movies are filmed and where you can choose to totally immerse yourself in any character or experience that interests you.

Stop and think about that for a few seconds.

Many systems of thought—especially the more metaphysical, new age, or mystical ones—say Earth is a school. They say we come here to learn lessons, and as we learn them we're allowed to go to more advanced levels.

What do you think of when you think of a school? Tests? Pressure? Someone else grading or judging your performance? Someone else deciding what you will or will not study, what you will or will not learn or do? Someone else deciding your daily schedule, whether you graduate, stay where you are, or flunk out?

That idea doesn't make sense to me. I prefer the concept of an amusement park. What do you think of when you think of an amusement park? Consider Disney World in Orlando, Florida, for example. You can go there to study the cultures of other countries at Epcot Center. You can visit the educational pavilions to learn about the human body, Earth's oceans, imagination and creativity, technological innovations, and many other subjects. You can also experience rides and other attractions that scare you, make you laugh, smile, and get your adrenaline flowing.

You go to an amusement park purely out of choice, don't you? You usually go with people you enjoy being with. You go to have fun. You go to explore what you want to explore, do what you want to do, learn what you want to learn. You can go on all the rides or attractions, repeat them over and over again, anything you want. You go when you want to go and you leave when you want to leave. You can return at any time.

It's a totally different approach than a school and is the only approach that helps you discover and navigate The Invisible Path to Success.

When it comes to "real life" movies, we like dramas, comedies, romances, horror stories, adventure, action, thrillers—every kind of subject there is.

Go into a bookstore. There are titles on every conceivable subject. Look at all the things being explored, studied, discussed, and shared on the Internet.

Read the daily newspaper and monthly magazines. Watch or listen to the news. All over the world you see people exploring everything that can possibly be explored. You see people totally immersing themselves in every kind of experience imaginable.

Now think back to why you go to movies in the first place. The reasons were

- They're fun.
- They provide an escape from your daily routine.
- You learn and grow from them.
- You experience different points of view and have different experiences.

I call all these things your "inner experiences." Why? Because they all go on inside of you. Having fun is a feeling you have inside. Having an "escape" from your daily routine is a feeling that happens inside you. Learning, growing, and experiencing different points of view are mental experiences, thought experiences, and feeling experiences, and they happen inside you, too.

If you really think about it, you don't go to a movie, read a good novel, or go to a football game because of what you see with your eyes and hear with your ears. It really doesn't matter if you're seeing an action film, a drama, or a romance movie. It doesn't really matter if the novel is set in modern times or ancient times or if someone lives, dies, or makes a million dollars. It doesn't really matter if the football team scores ten points or fifty points.

What matters is what's happening in your inner experience—what you think, what you feel, and what you learn.

Stop and consider that for a few seconds. What goes on *inside* of you is more important to you than what goes on *outside* of you.

I used to teach this at seminars. I'd ask someone in the audience to tell me something they really wanted in their lives that they didn't have right now. People would say more money, a new job, a new house, a new car, a new relationship.

I'd then ask, if they got the thing they wanted, what would it give them? When I asked the question enough times and peeled away enough layers, it always came down to a feeling they really wanted—peace of mind, more self-confidence, a sense of adventure, happiness, love—the list went on and on.

It was always an inner experience they really wanted, and the money, job, house, car, or relationship was just a possible pathway to the inner experience. It's the same with you and me and everybody else.

I recently saw the movie *Twister,* which I really liked. I read a lot of reviews of the movie that criticized it for being unrealistic. Experts said it didn't reflect what really happens with tornadoes. You know what? It doesn't matter!

For the most part, people didn't care. They enjoyed what the movie created in their *inner experience.* That's why they went and why so many people enjoyed it.

That's why you came to Earth in the first place. That's all you're after in your life. Your purpose is

> *To totally immerse yourself in situations that interest you and to explore the inner experiences—the thoughts, feelings, and learnings—that result.*

When the Disney Corporation decided to build Disneyland in California and, later, Disney World in Florida, management got together and decided what rides and attractions they'd offer the public. They still meet from time to time to decide what new attractions to add or old attractions to update and remodel.

It's the same with us here on Earth. Everyone who was involved in the creation of this amusement park got together and decided what kind of "rides" and "attractions" would be offered—what kinds of three-dimensional, total immersion movie adventures would be offered.

Just like the folks at Disney, from time to time we add rides, eliminate rides, and update or remodel the old faithfuls.

Let me share another analogy. I've never been much of a baseball fan. If you are, please forgive me, I mean no offense. But I was talking to a friend of mine once who is a *huge* baseball fan. I was telling him I preferred football and basketball because there was more action, and they moved faster.

He told me lots of people misunderstand baseball. He said baseball is primarily a mental game. He said every time something happens in a baseball game—a strike, a ball, a foul ball, a hit, a walk, a strikeout, an out—everything changes. One set of possibilities goes away and a whole new set of possibilities is created.

He said what's exciting to him about baseball is mentally exploring the possibilities that come and go, to see what happens, to consider the question, "What would happen if?"

The purpose and daily flow of your life are the same as my friend's view of baseball.

People all over the planet, no matter what they're doing or exploring, are fascinated by the possibilities. They're fascinated to see "What would happen if?" in all kinds of situations.

Look at history. In just about every area of human experience, things are being explored at deeper and deeper levels. Everything is evolving. Things are getting more and more sophisticated—in sports, business, politics, relationships, everything—as more and more "What would happen if?" scenarios are played through and the results shared.

Everyone is equal—in power, intelligence, and creative ability. If someone has more money than you, appears smarter than you, or appears to be a better athlete, a better musician, or a better businessperson, it's because they chose those circumstances, or they chose to develop those skills so they could explore what they wanted to explore.

It was a simple decision, and then the movie-making machine (which we'll be talking about later) clicked in and created their situation for them.

You could have created the same exact experiences for yourself. You still could—if it interests you enough.

There are people who've chosen to explore themes such as race, politics, power and money, psychology, spirituality, enlightenment, or proficiency, where they work hard to become really good at something like basketball, playing the piano, being a heart surgeon, being a writer—the list is endless.

Many people say the purpose of life on Earth is to become enlightened or spiritual. Other people say the purpose of life is to love or serve others. Still others say the purpose of life is to be happy.

There are a million different opinions and they're all valid, but they're just one movie theme, just one set of possibilities you can choose from. There are billions of other options.

Do you remember a movie called *Splash* with Tom Hanks and Darryl Hannah? If you've never seen it, I strongly suggest you go out and rent it. I really liked it. It was about a mermaid who comes up to the ocean's surface and lives out of the water for a while.

She knew very little about how our "surface" world worked. In one scene, she's watching an old western on television. She sees a cowboy being shot and dying. The mermaid, not understanding about television, starts to cry. The Tom Hanks character walks in, sees her crying, and asks her what's wrong.

She points to the television and explains about the cowboy. Tom Hanks says something like, "Oh no, he didn't really die. He's just an actor. It's make-believe. It's all illusion. The same actor will probably die on another show next week."

After she understands, the mermaid feels much better and stops crying. She even starts laughing.

Ralph Waldo Emerson once said:

It is the secret of the world that all things subsist and do not die, but only retire a little from sight and afterwards return again. Nothing is dead; men feign themselves dead, and endure mock funerals and mournful obituaries, and there they stand looking out of the window, sound and well, in some new strange disguise.

I would suggest that your life is the same. You're on Earth totally immersed in the inner experiences that interest you—even if you don't understand it consciously.

You want to explore possibilities, see "What would happen if?" in a specific set of situations. Everyone else on the planet is doing the same thing, exploring what interests them, even if it doesn't interest you, and even if you don't understand how anyone could possibly be interested in exploring such a thing.

You're born and the "filming" starts. You experience what you want to experience, then you die and the filming stops—for this particular movie anyway. Just like the cowboy in the *Splash* movie, it's all illusion. All props and special effects. All designed to create the *inner experiences* you want to explore.

Now, as you consider this idea, please remember that the first step was to

Let go of opinions
and use what works for you.

I don't know if the earth is really a special movie theater where three-dimensional, total immersion movies are filmed. But it doesn't matter.

What I discovered for myself and what I hope you'll discover for yourself, is that looking at life *as if it were* a three-dimensional, total immersion movie experience works!

By that I mean it's useful. It offers lots of benefits and can help you produce the results I think you want in your life. You'll know more about "how" by the time you reach the end of the book.

I've explained this approach to people from all over the world. Few people have trouble accepting it as possible or useful when they look at the more positive or exciting experiences in life—like being a millionaire, a movie star, a star athlete, Mozart, president of the United States, or Mother Theresa.

But they sometimes do have trouble accepting this possibility when it comes to the "darker" or so-called "negative" experiences like being a drug addict, a criminal, a murderer, or being poor or struggling with illness, a child dying young, being discriminated against because you're a so-called minority, and so on.

You and I could debate this very charged subject for weeks, but for now, since this is such an important part of the book, let me share the following thoughts.

If you take everyone on the planet together as a whole and look at the movies we watch, the books we read, and the stories we follow in the news, you'll see that we're interested, sometimes mesmerized, by stories about saints and sinners, "good" people and "evil" people, and "positive" and "negative" things. Much as we might hate to admit it, we're fascinated by everything that's happening, regardless of how we label it.

Going back to "real-life" movies for a second, I love fast-paced action movies, but my wife, Cecily, doesn't. She hates the killing and violence. Some people like horror movies with lots of blood, guts, gore, and what I consider terrible cruelty. I can't stand that kind of movie.

We're all different and what interests one person doesn't interest, and may even disgust, another—but that's the way life is.

There are billions of people on Earth who grew up in completely different places, had totally different educations, experiences, mentors, and teachers. They all look at the world from different perspectives and all came to this amusement park to explore different inner experiences in the first place.

So let me ask you this: If people are interested enough about so-called light and dark, good and evil, right and wrong, and positive and negative to read books, watch movies, or follow the news about them, is it such a stretch to think they might want to experience total immersion movie experiences with the same subjects?

Or ask yourself this question: Why, besides the money, would an actor or actress want to act out a dark, evil, or negative role? Think of Anthony Hopkins playing the role of an insane cannibal in the movie *Silence of the Lambs*—a hugely successful film from a few years back.

Think about the best-selling Stephen King horror stories that became successful movies. Think about any of the other so-called "dark" stories you've seen, read about, or heard about.

What's the answer? Because it interested him—even if it doesn't or couldn't interest you.

It's the same with the things you see happening all over the world. No matter what it is, no matter how you feel about it, someone else is so interested in the subject that they want to explore it more deeply by reading a book, following a news story, watching a movie, acting in a movie, or even having a total immersion movie experience to explore it at the deepest possible level!

I was at a party many years ago in Denver, Colorado. It was during the war in Iraq, just after all the news about the torturing of our soldiers came out. A woman at the party was shaking her head and saying, "I just don't understand how someone could be so cruel as to do that to another human being."

Strange as it might seem from one perspective, from another perspective, that woman might choose a total immersion movie experience one day where she's the one doing the torturing—so she can find out how someone could end up doing something like that to another human being.

There are many more examples like this to explain why people are so interested in exploring negative experiences. At seminars and in person, when I explain this phenomenon, many people say to me, "If I was choosing something to explore, I'd never choose the life I have now. Things are awful. I don't like the life I have now."

If a thought like that crosses your mind, please remember that you're only part of the way through your movie. You're in the middle of just one scene and you don't know where the movie is headed or where you'll end up.

The average movie these days is just under two hours. Have you ever seen a movie where at the forty-minute point the main character was in deep trouble, but then twenty minutes later everything was okay or things had changed a lot?

Remember the baseball story I told you. Every time something happens in your life—you go right or left at a fork in the road, you choose to do or not to do something, you make a decision—all the possibilities change and it's a whole new ball game.

It's the same with your life. You wouldn't judge a movie based on what was happening in one scene. You wouldn't judge a football game by what was happening in the second quarter. You might not even judge it by what was happening in the last two minutes. You wait until it ends and you've experienced the whole thing.

I'd suggest it's very valuable to look at your life the same way.

So life is about creating outer situations that allow you to explore the inner experiences that really interest you, even if they don't interest someone else. This is why there might always be crises, challenges, and problems for us here on Earth. They give us great opportunities to explore and experience!

This is also why I'm so optimistic about the future. When the time is right, when we're done exploring what we want to explore as a group, individuals will choose to have total immersion movie experiences to help us solve the problems we worry about most right now.

This is also why I think we love movies so much as a culture: on some level, we recognize it's a metaphor for what our lives are really about. It reminds us of what we're really doing here.

Now let's take a look at the nuts and bolts of how this total immersion movie model works. Before a movie is filmed, preparatory work has to be done. If you were going to produce a movie, the first thing you'd have to do is look at everything that's possible and write or buy a script on a subject that interests you. Next, you have to hire a *director* (who manages everything from behind the scenes), a *cast* (actors and actresses to play the various roles), and a *crew* (assistants that support the director in managing all the behind the scenes details).

Then you have to go to a studio or on location (or both) to start filming. Eventually, the movie is released, people see it and have their inner experiences.

It's the same with *your* life. Who you really are is much greater than who you might think you are right now. I use two words to describe who I think you really are. The first word is "star" and the second word is "director."

I call the person you think you are, the person who's reading my words right now, the "you" who's here on

Earth having a total immersion movie experience, the "star."

But there's another part of you, another aspect of *your consciousness* that you don't see, a part of you that's much more powerful, much more aware, and much older and wiser. From an off-Earth, much broader perspective, this other part of you took a look at Earth's amusement park and chose a subject you wanted to have a total immersion movie experience with.

That part of you assigned itself the role of writer, producer, and director of your total immersion movie experience. As a result, I call this part of you "the director." Other systems of thought call this your Higher Self, your Greater Self, or your Inner Being.

The parts of yourself you'd label "unconscious" or "subconscious" are what I call your movie crew or your staff of assistants.

The director is you, the crew is you, and the star of your movie is you. It's just different parts of the same individual, the same being, the same energy—whatever you want to call it—that have been split off and given different roles.

Think of what an actor does. Take Tom Hanks. Tom Hanks has a private life. He's married. He has a family. He does lots of things besides act. But when he chooses a movie role to play, like *Forrest Gump*, while he's on camera, he temporarily puts the real Tom Hanks on hold, steps into another character, and becomes that character for a while. When the shooting is over, he goes back to his real life.

So just like Tom Hanks accepts a role, you accept a role. Just like Tom Hanks temporarily shifts his focus to become another character, splits off part of himself (so to speak) to do it, so do you. And the director part of you manages everything from behind the scenes—just like the director of a "real" movie.

Once you have the theme, director, star, and crew for your movie, you've then got to "write" the script your movie will be based on. You create a master plan, if you will, that outlines what your goals are and what's going to happen.

Some movies are based on very detailed, long, and complex scripts that are rigidly followed, scene by scene, exactly as they were written. Other movies have more loosely defined scripts that change a lot after the movie production begins.

It's the same with you. You may have written a very detailed script for your movie experience—in advance—and you're following it line by line. Or you might have allowed for a lot of freedom and decided to make a lot up as you went along. It all depends on what you came to experience and how you wanted to experience it.

In my own case, for this lifetime, I believe I came in knowing this would be a fascinating time in history with lots of opportunities for exploration and growth. I believe I wrote a loosely defined script—a script in which I predefined certain things but left a lot up to choice once I was here and saw how things developed and emerged.

Once you have a script to guide you, you move on to the next step, which is to hire the rest of the cast. The word goes out, actors and actresses come, you audition and hire them to play major and minor roles in your total immersion movie.

They might play the role of mother, father, teacher, spouse, brother, sister, friend, or a stranger you meet only once on a bus but who impacts you in some deep way. These other actors and actresses, who themselves come down here to explore what interests *them,* agree to play a role in your movie for their own reasons. It's all choice, all agreement, and everyone benefits.

Once people accept roles in your movie, they agree to say the things, do the things, and have the impact on you that you want for your experience. You agree to do the same for them.

When you watch a movie, nothing happens by chance. Everyone and everything are there because the writer or director put them there to impact your inner experience in a certain way. It's the same with your life.

Think about the movies you see today. Tens of millions of dollars are spent. Thousands of people are involved. Months, sometimes years, of work go into the hour and a half or two hours you see on screen.

It's the same with your life. Tremendous resources are being invested behind the scenes to create your life just as it is. Everything you see around you—the buildings, nature, cars, houses, everything else—represents a prop or a special effect. It's all designed to impact you in certain ways so you can have the inner experiences you want to have.

Everything that happens to you, all the people you meet, and all the events that cross your path; all are managed, created, or allowed by your director so you can have the total immersion experience you want to have—so you can explore what you want to explore.

Actors and actresses don't usually concern themselves with the behind-the-scenes details on a movie set. They let the director and crew take care of them. They just step on stage, play their parts, and step off again.

When you go to a movie, do you want to be bothered by lots of details, or do you want to just sit in your seat and experience it? Do you want to know how a roller coaster works mechanically, or do you want to just ride it and have your experience? I believe it's the inner experiences you're after, not the details.

Once all the preparatory work is done, you're "born" and filming starts. You experience what you want to experience. When you die, the filming for this movie experience stops.

Sometimes in the movies, actors have big roles in long movies. Sometimes they have smaller or supporting roles. Sometimes they have what are called cameo appearances, where they appear on the screen for a scene or two. Sometimes there are sequels where the same character explores different adventures along similar lines.

It's the same with life on Earth. This is what my wife calls a "charged" subject, which means there's a strong possibility for disagreement or controversy. I explore this subject more fully through the books, tapes, courses, and special reports that complement this book, but for now let me say this. . .

Some people come here and by choice live long lives; others come here and by choice live short lives. Some people, just like movie actors, put in cameo appearances where they're here for a very short period of time, perhaps to help someone else with their movie experience or to receive some other benefit for themselves.

Sometimes there are sequels in Earth life too. Sometimes people have too much to explore for one total immersion experience, so they have a lot of related experiences until they explore everything they want to explore.

Whenever I think about this, I think of Mozart. Here you have the story of someone who began composing some of the world's greatest music as a child. Is it reasonable to assume he was born with that ability, or is it more likely that he devoted a series of total immersion movie experiences to exploring the world of musical composition and fine tuning his abilities until it culminated in the tremendous skill we know so much about?

Carl Jung, the famous psychologist, said:

My life as I lived it had often seemed to me like a story that has no beginning and no end. I had this feeling that I was a historical fragment, an excerpt for which the preceding and succeeding text was missing. I could well imagine that I might have lived in former centuries and there encountered questions I was not yet able to answer, that I had to be born again because I had not fulfilled the task that was given to me.

It's the same with you and me and everyone else. You may never know the reason a person chooses a certain role to play, an experience to explore, or what benefit he or she is getting from it—like in the case of a child dying in its first year, a young man or woman losing a leg, someone contracting a terrible disease, all the airplane and car "accidents" that claim lives—on and on.

It might be part of your movie to look at these events as tragedies. But it's also useful, and it also works, depending on what your goal is, to believe it was not an accident, not a tragedy, but the result of intelligence and planning.

It's also useful to believe it was all for a positive purpose and it benefited everyone involved even if you don't understand how it could have benefited someone from your own limited perspective.

You've heard me share my belief that it's useful to look at people who have an impact on you as actors playing roles you hired them to play. They're acting from a script you gave them to follow and dialogue you gave them to speak.

There are no victims, no matter how it looks or what people say. If you factor out death, pain, or accidents as bad, and factor in choice, purpose, or desire to explore because it interests someone (even if it doesn't interest you), things can look quite different.

You might find this hard to accept—particularly when looking at the so-called negative sides of life. If you do find it hard to accept, I ask you to consider this: Why is it so much easier to believe in victims, randomness, chaos, evil, win-lose scenarios, humans being powerless or weak little beings at the mercy of forces beyond our control than it is to believe in choice, purpose, intelligence, power, planning, and tremendous benefit for all involved?

Look at the world around you—the laws of physics, the way the planets and the sun orbit around the solar system, the amazing machine we call the human body, the way nature works. Everywhere you look, *if you look,* there's absolute brilliance to be seen. There's intelligence in action. You can see the latest buzzword, "synchronicity," at work.

Again, if you find this model hard to accept, I ask you: Why is it so hard to extend that brilliance, intelligence, purpose, and synchronicity to the events in your life?

A lot of effort was put into designing this amusement park we call Earth. A lot of effort goes into running it on a daily basis from behind the scenes. This cuts to the core of a question you must answer if you want true success in your life (whatever success means to you).

Sooner or later, you must answer the question: Is life random, or is there purpose and an intelligent plan? If you choose randomness, you'll always have fear, stress, and uncertainty. You'll never feel truly safe, comfortable, or confident in the world.

If you choose a purpose and intelligent plan, you at least have the possibility of feeling confident, strong, taken care of, safe, and a lot of other things I think you want to feel—depending on what your movie is about.

Since I believe in using what works, I choose the intelligent plan. What you choose is up to you.

Everything that happens in your life is shaped, molded, and determined at all times by these three questions:

1. What did I come here to explore?
2. How did I choose to explore it?
3. What is the bottom-line goal of my movie?

The answers to these three questions combine to create the first of the "unseen forces" that shape your life. I'll be talking more about this in chapter six.

William Shakespeare, in his play *As You Like It,* wrote:

All the world's a stage, and all the men and women merely players. They have their exits and their entrances, and one man in his time plays many parts.

Perhaps Shakespeare was even wiser than we gave him credit for—and we've given him a lot of credit!

You might find it extremely interesting to start looking at the lives of other people from this perspective—people you know, famous people, Olympic and professional athletes, other people whose lives you see dissected in books, movies, and the media.

A young man named Tom Dolan won a gold medal in swimming at the 1996 Olympics in Atlanta. He was considered by many people to be the best swimmer in the United States, if not the world. And yet he has trouble breathing. He had to overcome a lot of physical difficulties. And he pushed himself way beyond what many other athletes are willing to do.

It's a very inspiring story and an interesting example of how one person chose to manage the details of his movie script to explore what he wanted to explore.

Think about it. What might the breathing and health problems have set in motion in his *inner experience* that led to excellence in his sport, a gold medal, and other aspects of his life?

So what's this second step toward discovering The Invisible Path to Success? To

Take your seats to the best show in town.

The best show in town is the total immersion movie experience you came here to have. The seats you take are your inner experiences!

Consider how this perspective could change how you look at your life and how you look at what happens to you and everyone else as we prepare to take our third step together.

Chapter Three

The third step is what I call

Turn off the cruise control.

If you take a close look, your life, as complicated as it might seem, is composed of just two things—your inner experiences (what you think, what you feel, what you learn) and your outer experiences (what happens to you daily, the things you experience with your five senses).

In this third step, we're going to take a look at the unseen forces that shape your inner experiences. In step four, we'll take a look at your outer world. Then we'll go into detail on how you can better manage those unseen forces to get more of what you *really* want in your life.

As I mentioned in step two, when you decided to have your total immersion movie experience, things were set up so you'd be free to have your inner experiences without worrying about the details. By choice and design, you left management of the details up to your director and your unconscious crew of assistants.

All day long, thoughts fly in and out of your head. Feelings flow through your body. They're both triggered and shaped by a simple process that works very much like a computer.

Here's how it works. Whenever anything happens in your outer world—someone says something, someone does something, you hear something, you see something, you read something—whatever it is, the minute something happens, at the unconscious level, one of your assistants asks a very important question on your behalf:

What does this mean?

Your assistant then scans your memory banks, your beliefs, what you've learned, what you were taught, what's otherwise known as your "conditioning" or "programming," and attempts to answer the question.

After that, she then asks another important question:

How should I respond?

Based on how you answered the first question and the *meaning* you assigned your experience, you respond by thinking something, feeling something, or doing something as a result.

The other night my wife, Cecily, woke up and walked into our living room. As she looked over at the sliding glass door leading to the patio, she noticed it was open. She started to feel uncomfortable.

Why? Because she remembered closing and locking the door earlier in the evening. When she looked at the open door, one of her unconscious assistants asked, "What does this mean?"—then scanned her memory banks, past experiences, learning, conditioning, and programming, trying to answer the question.

Based on Cecily's past experiences, the conclusion her assistant drew was that someone might have broken in and was loose in the house. That started fear flowing. She woke me up and told me about the open door. At the unconscious level, the same process ran for me. My assistant asked, "What does this mean?"—and I concluded one of us probably left the door open after letting the dog out.

My assistant then asked, "How should I respond?" Based on the meaning I assigned to the open door, I felt no fear or discomfort, and I didn't feel motivated to do anything other than check the house, close the door, lock it, and do what I could to help Cecily feel better.

It was the same incident for both of us, but a radically different interpretation and a completely different set of thoughts and feelings as a result. All of this was driven by the simple process of asking and answering the two questions:

What does this mean?

and

How should I respond?

Let me give you a few more examples. When I say the word "divorce," what comes to your mind? What if I say the word "dog"? Or the word "money"?

What did you think, feel, even see in your mind's eye when I said those words? You probably went through the same process. I said the words "divorce," "dog," and "money." You heard the words and one of your unconscious assistants asked the question "What does this mean?" then scanned your memory banks. You then had thoughts, feelings, mental pictures, or whatever it was as a result of the second question, "How should I respond?"

I saw an article in the paper recently about a religious group that was upset with the Disney Corporation because it decided to give health care benefits to the spouses of homosexual employees. Since the religious group was against homosexuality, it publicly attacked Disney.

That may seem ridiculous to you. Perhaps you agree with the religious group. Whichever opinion you hold, it's driven by this machine-like asking and answering of two questions.

The interesting thing is that the asking and answering usually take place on autopilot without your conscious awareness or your conscious evaluation of the results.

It's the same process no matter what happens in your life—whether you're at work, driving, talking on the phone, playing with your kids, discussing current events with your spouse, reading, or watching a movie.

It's so fast you don't even know it's happening, and the really interesting thing is most if not all of it is learned. In most cases, you don't come into this world knowing what things mean or how to respond to them. It's something you have to learn.

Let me give you two metaphors to make this really clear. First, think of a jukebox. You put in a quarter and push A-6. The jukebox "circuitry" asks, "What does A-6 mean?" It scans its memory banks and finds out it's a Kenny G record. Then it asks, "How should I respond?" It's programming says, "Put it on the platter and play it"—and that's what happens.

You only see the metal, the glass, the buttons, and the records on the jukebox, but hidden from view is the programming that tells the jukebox what to do and how to do it in response to the buttons you push.

An even better metaphor is the computer. Have you used a word processor? A few clicks of a mouse and you underline a sentence. A few clicks and you move a paragraph from point A to point B. Click here and the spelling gets checked.

When you use software, you only see the surface of the program. But behind the scenes is a series of little instructions called "code" that tell the computer what to do and how to do it in response to your mouse clicks and keyboard typing.

When you click your mouse and make your selections, nothing would occur if your selections didn't activate these hidden instructions that make everything happen.

Once it's set up or programmed, the whole process goes on automatic and works the same way over and over, day after day.

Unless you change the programming, the jukebox will always play the Kenny G record when you push A-6. Unless you change the computer code, the word processor will always underline the sentence if you highlight it and click the right button.

I have an electronic dictionary on my computer. It was programmed to work a certain way. I type in a word and the definition flashes on the computer screen. Whenever I type in the word, I see the same definition on my screen. It's very mechanical and predictable. It's like the story of Pavlov's dogs who were conditioned to salivate when a bell rang.

It's the same with you. Your experiences program, teach, and condition you, and you often respond on "automatic" with thoughts and feelings when people push your "buttons" or ring certain "bells" in your life.

The minute you're born, the "programming process," the writing of unconscious instructions that tell you what things mean and what you should think, feel, and do in response, starts—and it continues throughout your life.

In the case of a jukebox, the programming is done by an engineer of sorts. With software, a computer programmer does it.

In your case, the programming is created by the experiences you have in this life or in past lives—if you believe in them. You learn what to do, how to feel about things, and what to do in response to them based on what happens to you, the conclusions you draw, the decisions you make, and what you were taught by your family, teachers, mentors, or anyone and anything that had an impact on you as you grew up.

Just as a programmer uses her keyboard to type instructions into a computer that tell the computer what to do and how to do it, your experiences create little instructions, rules, and formulas that say, "When this happens, do that," and "When that happens, feel this way."

When you were a child, your programming was still being written and hadn't been locked into place yet. But as an adult, so much of your behavior is on autopilot now—just like the cruise control in your car.

With cruise control, you decide the speed you want to go and turn a knob or push a button. The car stays at that speed, and the cruise control system makes all kinds of adjustments to maintain your speed as you go up and down hills.

Consider, for example, how you learned to walk as a child. At first, walking was an enormous struggle that required all your energy and attention. Within a few months, the period of intense struggle passed.

As the ability to walk became increasingly automated, you began to focus your attention on other things—reaching, touching, climbing. In the same way, you've automated just about every facet of your daily life: walking, driving, reading, working, relating to others—even thinking and feeling.

So much now is habit and pattern instead of conscious choice and intention. We don't usually notice or appreciate how much we run on automatic—mostly because we live in an almost constant state of mental distraction. Our minds are constantly moving about at a lightning-fast pace, thinking about the future, replaying events from the past, engaging in inner role-playing, watching television, listening to music, on and on.

I'm sure you've heard this or something like it before, but here's the really interesting part. The programming that drives a lot of your life on autopilot isn't accidental or random. It's not there by mistake. What is most important, it's not bad or wrong. It also represents the second of the unseen forces that shape your life.

Who you are, the way you think, and the way you feel were all *chosen, created,* or *allowed* by your director so you'd become the kind of person you wanted to become; you'd react to your environment the way you wanted to react; and you'd have the inner experiences and total immersion movie experience you wanted to have.

Stop and consider that for a few seconds.

Remember, you came here to explore specific inner experiences. Your director uses your experiences and inner programming like a sculptor uses clay, an artist uses paint, or a writer uses words.

We're going to be talking a lot more about how to turn off your cruise control later in this book and in the other books that follow, but for now it's important to know that the time has come for you to turn it off in certain situations and start maintaining your "speed" more consciously.

A lot of your programming is good for you. It's helpful to you. It makes living your life smoother, easier, and less stressful. But there are areas where your programming no longer serves you, even if it did at one time. There are areas where your programming is now causing you pain, holding you back, getting in your way.

It's time to take back conscious control over the programming and conditioning that no longer serves you.

It's time to remember who you really are—beneath all the layers of programming and conditioning—beneath all the layers of what other people told you about who you *should* be, how you *should* act, and what you *should* feel and do.

It's time to bring your lifestyle, your work, your relationships—everything—into alignment with the real you.

In the past, it was okay for your programming to drive so much of your life on autopilot. It was part of the plan because that's how you were exploring things. But now everything is changing.

Now it's time to explore with more conscious awareness.

Now it's time to take the machine apart and put it back together the way *you* consciously decide you want it to run.

So what's the third step toward discovering The Invisible Path to Success?

Turn off the cruise control.

You now know that your inner experiences are shaped by the way you answer the questions "What does this mean?" and "How should I respond?" at the unconscious level.

Now let's look at what creates your *outer* experiences—what actually happens to you day-to-day on the screen of your total immersion movie experience.

Chapter Four

I call the fourth step

Reach out and touch someone.

In our daily lives, we have telephones, cellular phones, fax machines, computers, the Internet, televisions, radios, and satellites. They link us all together and allow us to communicate with each other. If we weren't able to communicate like this, our lives would be radically different and it would be very difficult to get anything done.

You came here to totally immerse yourself in the inner experiences that interested you. As we discussed, you chose to leave the day-to-day handling of the details to your director and unconscious crew of assistants.

To actually get your movie filmed and get the actors, actresses, and crew together to tell them what to do, how to do it, and when to do it, your director and crew also need access to a communications system at the unconscious level.

So when this total immersion movie studio called Earth was built originally, a very special unconscious communications network was added to the mix. This communications network connects all living things on the planet together at the unconscious level. If you know about computer networks or online services like the

Internet or America Online, it's similar but much bigger, more powerful, and infinitely faster—and you don't need a computer.

The concept of all living things being connected at the unconscious level was considered "new agey" or "way out" for lots of years, but it's now being documented by scientists all over the world.

A famous experiment was conducted many years ago. I totally disagree with what was done in the experiment, and I'm only sharing it with you because it dramatically illustrates an important point I want to make.

The researchers took a mother rabbit in this experiment and put her in a submarine they submerged off the coast of Japan. The mother rabbit was then wired to a bunch of fancy gizmos to measure her responses.

One of her baby rabbits, who was in California at the time—and this is the part I hate—was then killed at a prearranged time. At the exact moment the baby rabbit was killed in the United States, the mother, thousands of miles away, submerged in a submarine, went crazy. She knew!

When I was sixteen, at three in the morning, I was in a bad car accident in Milwaukee, Wisconsin. At the exact moment it happened, my sleeping mother woke up, shot straight upright in bed, and knew something "bad" had happened to me.

Think about the psychic experiences you've had or heard about—where you just knew something was going to happen before it happened. Or you somehow knew what someone else was thinking or what they were going to say before they said it. It's everywhere you look—if you look.

So we're all connected at the unconscious level, and all day long, *metaphorically,* we're sending classified ads into the network asking for what we want and offering to give what we want to give to others.

Twenty-four hours a day, seven days a week, these ads flash back and forth at the unconscious level. People respond to our ads. We respond to theirs. And just as in the "real world," we discuss, negotiate, and make agreements: "I'll do this for you if you'll do that for me." Then something happens on the surface in what we call our daily lives.

Everything that happens in your daily life is generated by this unconscious flow of classified ads. Everyone that comes into your life, everyone who's in your life right now, and everyone who has an impact on you, no matter how big or small, is there because of one or more of the following possibilities:

1. An ad you sent into the network.
2. An ad your director sent into the network on your behalf.
3. Someone else's ad your director responded to on your behalf.

This represents the third of the unseen forces that shape your life.

No matter what you want, no matter what experience your director wants to bring into your life, other people on the planet can and will help you create it.

Why? Because at the unconscious level, everyone knows we're here to explore and experience, and even though it doesn't usually look like it on the surface, everyone wants to help everyone else have the total immersion movie experiences they want.

Imagine, if you will, this gigantic planet of ours. Billions of people are running around filming their total immersion movies. They need actors and actresses to play certain roles in their scenes. They need certain things to happen in their daily lives. Classified ads are sent into the unconscious network and things happen in their lives as a result.

When I think about it, it gets me incredibly excited. It fascinates me, and I'm awed by the raw power at work and at our disposal every day. It's truly amazing.

If you're using the online services or the Internet, and you're excited about that, imagine magnifying the available resources and possibilities a billion times. Then you'll just be in the ballpark of what's possible with the unconscious network I'm talking about.

One very important thing you need to know about the unconscious network is that unless your director intervenes to change things (which often happens), the one guideline that applies is

All ads sent into the network will be
taken literally by the people reading them.

No one second-guesses you. No one tries to read between the lines. No ones tries to figure out what you mean. Everything is taken literally.

This is one of the reasons why so many people don't receive what they ask for when they use personal development techniques. Their director would have allowed their request, but something in their ad that's taken literally at the unconscious level interferes with them getting what they asked for.

Let me give you some specific examples to illustrate this. I once did a private consultation with a woman we'll call Sarah. Sarah had a dream that she was not fulfilling. Her dream was to go to China to teach Chinese kids English and American entrepreneurialism as China becomes more of an active participant in world affairs.

The problem was that she didn't speak Chinese. She knew of a special school where she could become fluent rather quickly, but the course cost $5,000 and she didn't have the money.

She knew she could borrow the $5,000, but then she worried that if she borrowed it, became fluent in Chinese, and traveled to China—no one would want to study with her, or she wouldn't be able to find a decent place to live, or she wouldn't make any friends and she'd be halfway around the world, alone and in debt. Then she'd become scared and back off.

I listened to her for a while and then I asked her, "What do you think the ad you're sending into the unconscious network says?"

She paused, then laughed and said: "It probably says something like, 'Wanted: Help to travel to China to live my dream. Need $5,000. But what if I get there and no one wants to study with me? Or I can't find a decent place to live? Or I don't make any friends? Oh, this is too scary. I don't know if I really want this at all.'"

I looked at her and said, "No one could possibly respond to that ad. It's not asking for anything. And that's why you're not going to China."

In reality, she wanted help getting the $5,000. She wanted help finding students. She wanted help finding a decent place to live and making friends. And she wanted help to overcome her fears. But her ad didn't actually ask for help in these areas, and the final sentence questions whether she even wants any help at all. Since everything sent into the network is taken literally, she could not receive the help she needed, and she wasn't going to China.

I suggested she send another ad into the network that read something like this:

> *Wanted: Support in traveling to China to live my dream.*
> *I'd like help raising $5,000 to take a Chinese fluency course.*
> *Then, once I arrive, please help me find a lot of students to*
> *work with, a nice place to live, and some really good friends.*
> *Finally, since I'm both excited and a bit afraid of this, please*
> *help me come to terms with my fears and overcome them.*

That ad is clear. It's asking for something. When it's taken literally, people can and will respond to offer assistance—if it's part of her movie.

I'll give you another example. I did a private consultation with a young man we'll call Brent. Brent had been in the same job for twelve years and he hated it. He didn't always hate it, but he hated it now, and he desperately wanted to make a change.

The problem was that he didn't know what he wanted to do instead. He spent hours wondering if he should go into insurance sales or become a fireman, a computer repair technician, or a cab driver. And he wasn't getting any offers that appealed to him. He was frustrated.

I said to him, "Forget what the ideal next job for you will look like. Have you thought about what job *elements* will make you happy? What do you really like to do? Do you want to be inside or outside? Eight to five or flexible hours? Work with a lot of people or mostly by yourself? Fast paced with lots of excitement or slow paced and calm? How much money do you want to make ?"

He interrupted me and said, "Look, I just want to survive. I just want to know my bills are paid."

"What does that mean in dollars and cents?" I asked him.

"About $2,000 a month."

"Guess what your ad says?" I asked him. "I hate my job. I don't know what I want to do instead, but I need something that will pay me about $2,000 a month so I can survive and pay my bills."

That ad, or something like it, was going into the network. People were responding, and he was being offered jobs that paid in the range of $2,000 a month—jobs that didn't appeal to him.

In reality, he didn't want a job that paid him $2,000 a month. He'd been making more than that in his old job. What he really wanted was a job that paid $2,000 a month, as a minimum, but preferably more.

Since his ad is taken literally at the unconscious level, if he asks for $2,000 a month, that's what he'll receive job offers for. If someone has a job that could really make him happy and pays $2,500, $5,000, or $10,000 a month, *they won't respond to his ad.*

Also, since his unconscious staff of assistants take his ads literally too (unless his director intervenes), they will ignore the other ads in the network that offer jobs paying more than $2,000 a month too.

I suggested that Brent do three things:

1. Send an ad into the network asking for help to clarify the kind of job that would make him happy.
2. Spend some time consciously thinking about the job *elements* he thought would make him happy.
3. Send another ad into the network asking for the job elements he thought would make him happy, but asking for $2,000 *or more* in monthly earnings.

I'll give you one last example of how the Universe, taking your unconscious ads literally, can produce interesting results. I did a private consultation with a fifty-year-old woman I'll call Billie. Billie had a successful real estate career; was beautiful, sweet, intelligent, and warm; had two wonderful kids she adored. The only thing that had always been missing from her life was a really great relationship with a man.

I told her about the unconscious network, the ads that shape what happens to us, and the need to be very clear in what she asks for.

"I know that," she said. "I've written ten pages about what I want my man to be like and what I want us to be like, but I keep drawing in these wackos."

I had an intuitive flash about what might be causing the problem, so I said, "Close your eyes and take a deep breath. Now, take yourself back in time to when you wrote those ten pages about your ideal man. Can you do that? Can you go back there and see what you were seeing, feel what you were feeling, hear what you were hearing—really be there?"

"Yes," she said.

"Okay. Now, as you finish writing the tenth page, is there anything else going on? Are you saying anything to yourself, feeling anything, hearing anything?"

She paused. Then she opened her eyes and started to cry.

"You know what it is?" she asked me.

"No," I said. "What is it?"

"I finish writing and then I say to myself, 'A guy like that wouldn't want me.'"

Boom! Just like that, a "P.S." goes into her ad and changes everything. Since her ad will be taken literally at the unconscious level, the "right men" will be reading her ad and saying "I fit that. I do that. That's how I am." Then they'll read her P.S., take it literally, and not respond to her ad. In this case, her P.S. is like a command telling them to go away.

Are you beginning to see how powerful this taking things literally at the unconscious level can be?

So often we send ads into the network that aren't clearly asking for what we want (like Sarah and her China dream). Or our ads are clear (like Brent asking for $2,000 a month), but they're not what we really want. Or our ads are clear and for what we really want, but a P.S. gets added that undercuts or "cancels" the ad.

What I call "self-talk" can also be turned into ads or P.S.'s that repel things from you or bring things into your life you don't want—consciously.

If you often say things to yourself like, "I'm so stupid," or "I can't do anything right," or "This always happens to me," or "I always do that," those self-talk messages, if allowed by your director, can go into the network and have an impact on your life. As we've seen, if allowed by your director, they can also be taken as commands that your unconscious crew of assistants obey without question.

Finally, very often, when something happens in your life, your "What does this mean?" and "How should I respond?" machine runs on autopilot at the unconscious level, the questions are answered, and the answers result in an ad, a series of ads, a P.S. in an ad, or a series of P.S.'s in ads that go into the network without your even knowing about it.

If you've been wondering why you, or someone you know, keeps repeating the same patterns over and over, making the same "mistakes" over and over—like accepting the same kind of dead-end job, being mistreated or abused in personal relationships, making and losing money, on and on—unconscious communication and the flow of unconscious classified ads are what causes it.

To support you in having your total immersion movie experience, your director sends or allows the same kinds of ads into the network. Different people—or your own unconscious staff of assistants—respond to them, different agreements are made, and you have the same experiences over and over in your life.

Until I started navigating The Invisible Path to Success, I could never understand why certain patterns repeated themselves in my life.

Many years ago, I drew the same kind of woman into my life three times in a row—a woman who wanted to take but didn't know how to give. So I gave and gave and gave and got very little back.

After a while, I became exhausted and started resenting what was going on. Then I started making demands, which weren't met, and I'd finally end the relationships in what turned out to be messy and painful ways.

In each case, although the women had different backgrounds, looks, voices, names, and jobs, they were carbon copies of each other in how they acted and how they treated me.

"How could that possibly happen?" I wondered. "Of the billions of people out there, how could I draw the exact same kind of person into my life three times in a row like that?"

There were other people I knew who could walk into a room with 300 people in it, 299 of whom were psychologically "healthy," and one of whom was psychologically "unhealthy," and they'd instantly be attracted to the one "unhealthy" person in the room. "How could they do that time after time?" I wondered.

There were other patterns in my life as well. I could never understand how I kept repeating the same career pattern over and over, where I'd be offered a great job opportunity, take it, do a good job, and become increasingly successful. Then suddenly, out of nowhere, something strange would happen and everything would fall apart, leaving a big mess to clean up both emotionally and financially.

Another pattern I repeated was always being ignored in restaurants by waiters and waitresses who seemed to be giving everyone else great service. It was eerie.

Why were these things happening? I drew the same kind of woman into my life because an ad that went into the network (heavily influenced by self-esteem issues and programming I was struggling with at the time) specifically requested them.

These women treated me the way they did because unconscious communication through the network (and between our directors) asked them to. All along, they were just doing what I was asking them to do at the unconscious level.

Why did I create such ups and downs in my career? I had a father who was very successful financially when I was growing up, but he achieved his success at great expense.

He had cancer, heart disease, horrible headaches called "cluster headaches," which are even worse than migraines, and insomnia. Because he was so consumed by his work and traveled so much, his relationship with my mother suffered, as did his relationships with me, my brother, and my sister.

Witnessing this as a kid, I made a decision that if you become too successful, you'll hurt everyone around you, including yourself. That became part of my programming and part of what was sent into the network at key times without my knowing it consciously.

I wanted success in my life, so ads went into the network asking for great opportunities. I got them. I became more and more successful. Then, as I was about to become unbelievably successful, the programming about success leading to pain would click in. My director would allow it because it was part of what I was exploring at the time, and a new set of ads would go into the network, causing a series of experiences that resulted in everything crashing down upon me.

It was the same thing with being ignored in restaurants. I had programming at the time that said "people always ignore me." As a result, ads went into the network, in effect, asking the waiters or waitresses to ignore me, even if they were giving other people great service and would have given me great service too. But taking the ad literally and wanting to give me what I was asking for, they complied and ignored me.

Can you identify with these kinds of patterns in your life and what might be causing them?

Once I discovered The Invisible Path to Success and started changing the ads I was sending into the network (and the unconscious requests I was making of my director and assistants) everything started to change for me.

Another important feature of the unconscious communications network is that at the unconscious level there are no secrets. In our daily conscious lives, we keep things secret from other people. We hold things back. Sometimes we have a hard time opening up, getting to know other people or letting them get to know us. Some people even lie about things or distort the truth.

Behind the scenes, your director, and everyone else's director, knows everything about everyone—and they're constantly talking to each other as they work to create the total immersion movie experiences we all want.

When you communicate with other people by phone, in person, or by letter, advertisement, radio, or television, you might think they only know what you tell them, but the truth is, at the unconscious level, we're all open books. This is what I call

The secret force that governs all relationships.

At the unconscious level, our directors know everything, but from time to time (more often for some than others) they allow some of that knowledge to flow up to your conscious mind in what you experience as hunches, thoughts, feelings, insights, or intuition—all of which can have an impact on you.

If you've ever had a psychic reading or consulted a channel and they knew something about you or predicted something that ended up coming true, this is how they did it. They tapped into the unconscious network to find information about you—or they "talked" to your director.

Examples of your tapping into the unconscious network or getting a message from your director include the following: when you know what someone is going to say before they say it, you know something is going to happen before it happens, or you know who's calling before you pick up the phone.

When you meet individuals for the first time and have very strong feelings about them—you're attracted to them, you like them, you feel comfortable with them, you feel you can trust them, or you don't like them, you don't feel comfortable with them, or you don't feel you can trust them—you're receiving information about them through the unconscious network or from your director.

To find The Invisible Path to Success and start navigating where you want to go, you must understand that this communication is taking place behind the scenes. Unconscious communication is shaping your experiences, determining who comes in or out of your life, what kind of impact (if any) they have on you, the impact you have on them, and the various *outer* experiences that create the *inner* experiences you're here to explore.

It's also important to learn to work with the network more consciously to find out what ads you're sending into the network and what P.S.'s are attached to them.

It's important for you to understand the nuts and bolts of how to make the asking process as effective as possible and how the unconscious network really works. It's important for you to understand how to make changes in all these areas so you can start getting different results in your daily life.

The phone company ads tell you to reach out and touch someone using the telephone lines. When navigating The Invisible Path to Success, you use the unconscious network to reach out and touch your director, your crew of assistants, and the people who can help you create what you really want in your life!

This is the fourth step.

Chapter Five

The fifth step is what I call

Tap all your resources.

For as long as I can remember, I've been a very analytical person. From the time I was a kid through age thirty-five, I tried to live my life exclusively by intellect and logic. I analyzed everything, thought through everything, and tried to do the logical thing at all times. If you're a *Star Trek* fan, I tried to be like Spock.

I consider myself to be a bright guy—but you know what I learned by trying to live my life that way all those years? I learned that it doesn't matter how smart you are, how logical you are, or how hard you try, you can't succeed in life by intellect, thinking, or logic alone. It doesn't work. It's not a successful strategy.

Why? Three reasons:

1. There are exceptions, but in general, your "analytical skills" (your brain) aren't powerful enough to process all the information it takes to make a solid decision.

   Life is too complicated. There's too much going on, too many details and variables to consider, too many options and possibilities. As powerful as your analytical skills can be, they just aren't powerful enough.

2. Even if your analytical skills were powerful enough to process all the information it takes to make a solid

decision, you don't know enough. There's too much you don't know and don't see.

With few exceptions, you don't know what your movie is about, where you're headed, what this particular scene is about, or what your upcoming scenes will be about.

You don't know—consciously—which people (out of the billions to choose from) could be the most helpful to you. You don't necessarily know—consciously—what job would be best for you, what mate would be right for you, whether a big business deal going through or not going through would be the best thing for you, and so on.

You see lots of people around you, but you have no idea what *their* total immersion movies are all about. When someone comes into your life, you don't necessarily know—consciously—what they want from you in a certain scene or what you want from them in a certain scene.

You see so little of what's on the surface, much less what's going on behind the scenes where your director and crew live and work. That's the way it was designed to be. Remember, it's about *total immersion* in your movie experience.

3. Even if your analytical skills were powerful enough to process all the information and even if you did have access to enough information, the minute you get your hands around a big enough piece of information to make a decision, the world changes and your information may or may not be accurate or relevant anymore.

Decisions are being made every second throughout the world. Once a decision is made anywhere, all the possibilities change for all of us. Everything changes. Remember the baseball analogy.

Don't get me wrong—logic, intellect, and analytical skills are very powerful tools. But they've got to be looked at for what they are—tools—and their limitations must be seen clearly.

70

This all ties to step one and further explains why you may never know the absolute truth about anything and why it's so important to experiment and use what works for you.

It's incredibly useful to supplement your analytical skills by tapping the additional resources at your disposal—namely, the unconscious network, your director, and your unconscious crew.

Even though your analytical skills aren't powerful enough, the skills your director has are. Remember, he's a much more powerful part of you and has access to much more information. He's also smarter than you could ever hope to be in Earth form.

He knows everything about you—what your movie is about, what the goal is for your current scene and for upcoming scenes, where you're headed, etc. He knows why everyone else is in your life and what they were asked to do in their auditions. He has access to the network to find out anything else he needs to know about anyone or anything in your life.

For these reasons, your director is also able to manage the continuously moving target of a world where things are changing all the time. It just makes sense to tap such an incredible resource as much as possible to live your daily life.

In our world, we have had many so-called geniuses. What is a genius? Someone who either has knowledge you don't have or someone who has the ability to process information better, faster, or more creatively than you do. Isn't that all a genius really is?

You too have access to genius when you tap into the additional resources available through your director and the unconscious network—instead of just using your mental, analytical, logical, or intellectual skills.

Sometimes we get so caught up in the outer world that we forget to allow the inner world in. Let it in. There's so much power there.

Through your director's involvement in your life from behind the scenes, you tap many of these resources without knowing it. What I'm suggesting is that you do it more often, more directly, and more consciously.

As I mentioned earlier, to communicate in our world we use cellular phones, television, radio, fax machines, satellite dishes, telephones, modems, etc. All these things are based on numbers and frequencies. If you want to reach someone by phone, fax, or modem, you've got to know the number to dial. To pick up a television station, radio station, or satellite channel, you've got to tune a receiver to a particular frequency.

All the communication flashing back and forth through the unconscious network operates at certain frequencies too. You can learn to dial those "numbers." You can learn to tune your own "receiver" to those frequencies and connect directly to your director, your crew, and the unconscious network.

We give this process names like intuition, inner guidance, psychic insight, and sixth sense.

Albert Einstein once said:

> *The really valuable thing is intuition. The intellect has little to do on the road to discovery. There comes a leap in consciousness, call it intuition or what you will, and the solution comes to you and you don't know how or why.*

In the old days, if you talked about intuition, psychics, inner voices, or a guiding presence, people thought you were crazy. Today, it's gaining more acceptance.

Intuition is being openly cultivated by professionals from financiers to filmmakers, doctors, lawyers, executives, teachers, therapists, scientists, artists, public servants, and others to enrich their lives. Best-selling books are being written about people who use it. Hit movies are featuring characters with it.

Why? Because it works!

Why is intuition so valuable? Because anything that happens in your conscious daily life passes through your "What does this mean" and "How should I respond?" machine and gets colored by your programming. Intuition comes straight through from your director, your crew, or the network—and it isn't colored by memory, your experience, or your programming.

I believe that intuition, psychic ability, or inner awareness, whatever you want to call it, is the ultimate power. How do you develop it? There are lots of books, tapes, and courses out there. Perhaps one is right for you.

Or, if it interests you, send an ad into the network asking for guidance to the people, resources, ideas, and opportunities that can help you develop this critical ability. I'll be showing you how to write and send ads into the network later in the book.

Until you develop your own intuitive skills, I recommend using good psychics to help you develop them or as confirmation as you learn to trust yourself.

Like everything else, there are good psychics and not-so-good psychics. The key is finding the ones that are best for you. If you'd like a list of psychics I've personally worked with and can vouch for, please contact my office and request it (please see pages 164-165 for details).

Sometimes I think my life was saved by the psychics or "intuitives" I consulted. At times, I didn't know if I could go another day feeling as depressed, angry, confused, and unhappy as I did. No traditional source of information, or even my own mind at the time, was able to give me the answers these people gave me and I will be eternally grateful.

I'm also a big fan of meditating. Meditation is one of the most powerful ways you can open and develop a direct link to your director, your crew, and the unconscious network that links us all together. It's also one of the best ways to take more conscious control of your "What does this mean?" and "How should I respond?" machine.

There are lots of books, tapes, and workshops on meditating. I also discuss my personal experiences and recommendations in the next book in The Invisible Path to Success series.

When you think of the knowledge your director has, the knowledge the other directors have, and the additional knowledge and help easily available to you through the unconscious network, the raw power at your disposal is truly amazing! It's absolutely awe-inspiring.

Tap all your resources. That's the fifth step toward discovering The Invisible Path to Success.

Chapter Six

In many ways, this sixth step is one of the most important, because it explains why so many personal development systems fail to deliver the results you want.

I call the sixth step

You always get a vote, but you
don't always win the election.

If your director wants to create a certain scene in your movie, she sends ads into the network or responds to ads other people sent and negotiates until she gets what she wants for you. Then something happens in your life as a result. It's fairly cut-and-dry, simple, and it happens all day long, every day. A large percentage of your life's *outer* experiences are created by your director running or responding to ads on your behalf.

If you are doing the asking—through your thoughts, beliefs, feelings, fears, attitudes, intentions, and expectations—or by using techniques like goal setting, meditation, visualization, affirmations, etc.—it's a completely different story.

Any time you ask for something, the first thing that happens is that your request, whatever shape it takes, goes to your director for approval. The first question your director asks is

*Is this request in alignment with your movie
generally or the current set of scenes specifically?*

If the answer is no, your director pulls the ad and it doesn't go into the network. As a result, you won't receive what you asked for—no matter what you do, what technique you use, or how hard you try. What's most important to you is the overall, bottom-line movie experience you came here to have—not every conscious desire you may have along the way.

If the answer is yes, your request passes through a six-step process that determines what granting your request will look like and when you'll receive what you asked for.

Here are the six steps.

1. Your director determines whether a P.S. is in your ad. If there is one, he/she decides to keep it or delete it.

2. Your director sends your ad into the network, and it is taken literally by the Universe.

3. Your director fields responses, scans other ads, responds to them, negotiates, and makes agreements.

4. Your director determines how the granting of your request will actually look when it shows up in your life.

5. Your director determines what the best timing is for your request to be granted.

6. What you requested shows up in your life with the agreed-upon timing and shape.

So many books and approaches say you have unlimited power and you can create anything you consciously want. In fact, if you look closely, this theory cannot be supported by your actual day-to-day experience—no matter how good it sounds or how much you want to believe it.

Whenever I think of this subject, I think back to one of the original *Star Trek* episodes on television.

If you don't know about *Star Trek,* follow along because you'll get the idea anyway. In the episode, the senior crew of the star ship *Enterprise* were scouting a planet for the rest of the crew to vacation on.

Once they got to the planet, strange things started happening. People from the pasts of the senior crew started showing up. A huge tiger from the imagination of a crew member also showed up. An old propeller plane from the past of another crew member showed up and started firing machine guns at him. A fantasy of a female crew member, where she was a damsel in distress and saved by a knight in shining armor, came to life. On and on.

It was an amazing story. In one case, a crew member got hurt; in another, a crew member was actually killed by a character from his imagination who came to life. The crew didn't understand what was happening or why it was happening. Finally, it turned out the planet was a very special resort created by an advanced civilization. They had sophisticated technology that monitored your thoughts and a special factory that could create anything needed to make your thoughts real—even human look-alike robots.

Most people who came to that resort understood what it was. They controlled their thoughts and had a great time living out their fantasies or reliving fond memories. But since the *Star Trek* crew didn't know the real purpose of the planet or how things worked, their thoughts became dangerous.

If all your thoughts, feelings, fantasies, wants, and desires showed up in your life, or even just the ones you focused a lot on, your life would be total chaos. It would be an unstable, crazy, scary mess—just like it was for the people in the *Star Trek* episode—especially when you consider how often and how quickly you change your mind about things.

Plus, you'd never be able to have the total immersion experience you came here for, because your direction and experiences would change every few seconds without planning, order, or purpose.

Think about it.

So a system of checks and balances was put in place—where your director monitors everything, compares it to the bottom-line goal of your movie or the scenes currently being filmed, and filters what happens and what doesn't happen—for your benefit!

At this point, the question that usually comes up is, "If your director filters everything and decides what will happen in your life, do you have free will?" The simple answer is yes and no.

Some people build a lot of free will into their movie scripts; other people build in very little. It all depends on what your movie is about, what you came to explore, and how you wanted to explore it.

You have free will in the sense that your director is you, so no force outside of you is shaping things. You also have free will in the sense that it's your movie and you can experience anything you want to experience. You can change things at any time if you and your director change your minds about something.

But understand, when you decided to have your total immersion movie experience, you chose something that interested you; the minute you chose, you limited yourself.

Think of it this way. Suppose it's a Saturday afternoon and you want to go to a movie with your friend Sam. You scan the listings and decide to see *Independence Day*.

You could have gone to see any movie, but the minute you chose *Independence Day,* you limited yourself, closed doors, and cut off the possibility of seeing another movie in the same moment.

But you don't get upset about it because you made the choice. You know you chose to limit yourself. Plus, you know you can always go to another movie another day, so you didn't really lose anything.

I'd suggest it's the same with your life here. The minute you made the choice to have a total immersion movie experience, you wrote your script, hired your actors, and started filming when you chose to be born; you limited yourself to exploring certain experiences and not others.

You can certainly change your mind anytime, but it doesn't happen much because you wouldn't have picked a subject to explore and gone to all the trouble of writing a script, hiring actors and actresses, being born, and starting your adventure if you weren't absolutely committed to exploring that subject.

As a result, you tend to stay limited to exploring just a small part of what's available here on Earth in any one total immersion movie experience or lifetime.

What does this mean? It means that you have free will and unlimited power *in theory* but not in practice. It means there can be a huge difference between what you think you want, from the limited perspective of your conscious mind, and what you *really* want, from the broader perspective of your director, who wants to make sure you squeeze every last ounce of benefit from your explorations.

You always get a vote, meaning you can always ask for what you want and offer your opinion as to why you want it, but you don't always win the election, meaning you don't always receive what you ask for.

This is why some personal development techniques work for some people and not others; why they work sometimes and not other times. A technique will only work for you if getting what you've asked for, or getting it within your preferred time frame, is what I call "part of your movie."

The director part of you makes the decision—not the conscious part of you. Even though it might contradict what you presently believe, it's important to admit that

*Your conscious self is **not** running the show.*

It can look that way sometimes, but it's not the case. Plus, believing this often leads to frustration, anger, feeling cut off or disconnected, and even beating yourself up for being a failure or having done something wrong.

You can ask for anything you want, and as you'll soon see, I strongly recommend you ask for *everything* you want—from the smallest wish to the largest and most grand fantasy.

But I also suggest you be realistic about it and understand that you might not receive it. I also suggest that if you don't receive something you asked for, you look at it as good news, not bad news.

Why? Because if you don't get what you ask for, it's because it isn't what you really want, and when you do get what you really want, it'll be much better for you than what you think you want.

Now to be quite frank, the idea that you don't have as much free will as you thought you did bothers some people. It might bother you. If it does, let me plant a few seeds in your belief system that might grow into something valuable for you.

Some people resist this idea because they see an image of either being a puppet or being controlled by someone else, and that makes them feel small, weak, and insignificant. I look at it in exactly the opposite way.

If you're in an amusement park and you choose to go on the roller coaster, once you board the ride and get strapped in, someone else, so to speak, is in control of your experience. The roller coaster will go up and down at certain times, splash through water at certain times, and go right and left and upside down at certain times. You have no conscious control over it, but you don't care because you chose the ride. You knew you wouldn't have control and you wanted the inner experience anyway.

I would suggest it's the same thing with your life. You chose a set of inner experiences to explore. You asked the director part of you—not someone else—to manage the details so you could be free to have the experience you wanted.

The presence of your director as the part of *you* who filters things and takes care of things behind the scenes represents the fourth and final unseen force that shapes your life.

This is good news. As I hope you've seen from taking your first six steps, tremendous power and resources are being invested by your director every second of every day (even while you sleep) to make sure you get the total immersion experience you came here for.

That makes me feel good, safe. That makes me feel taken care of. That makes me feel much more confident in what can be viewed as a scary and unsafe world. Because I know all the power that's making everything possible is another part of me, I feel very powerful, very significant, very *big*.

Another reason why this makes me feel so good ties back to what we discussed earlier—that we see and know so little. I'm glad I'm not responsible for managing the details. I'm glad all my thoughts, beliefs, feelings, fears, attitudes, intentions, and expectations don't manifest in my life.

I'm glad the director part of me filters things and takes care of things behind the scenes. Why? Because while I have a healthy respect and opinion for my analytical skills, my conscious self, my value and worth, I also recognize that the conscious part of me isn't powerful enough or knowledgeable enough to do the job alone!

Does this mean you sit back and do nothing? Sometimes. Does it mean you don't ask for anything? Sometimes. Remember, there are no rules, no formulas. It all depends on what you came here to explore and what your movie is about.

Since I see so little, since I know so little, and since I know I can't always make solid decisions using analytical skills alone, I decided to change how I went after what I wanted in life.

I decided I'd just ask for what I want (knowing it's only what I *think* I want and not necessarily what I *really* want), and I'd let my director make the decisions, manage the details, and make most of the arrangements. I decided I'd just let go, trust my director, tap all my resources, and flow with what I felt strongly motivated to do as a result. We'll be discussing exactly how to do that in the next section of this book.

What's the sixth step toward discovering The Invisible Path to Success?

> *You always get a vote, but you*
> *don't always win the election.*

You've now been given a lot of pieces to the jigsaw puzzle I mentioned at the start of the book.

Hold on; just one more step, just a few more pieces, then the whole picture will pop into view and we'll start talking about how you can use all these ideas to get benefits in your daily life.

So with no further delay, let's move on to the seventh and final step.

Chapter Seven

I call the seventh step

Sail with the winds of change.

In the second step, you learned it was useful to look at life on Earth as if it were a three-dimensional, total immersion movie experience, and that all of us here are exploring the "What would happen if?" scenarios that interest us.

You learned that life is not really about what's happening in your *outer* experience, what you call your daily life, but the *inner* experiences that your outer experiences stimulate—what you think, what you feel, what you learn.

You discovered that from a broader, wider perspective, everyone (taken together as a group) who chooses to play in this Earth amusement park decides what movie themes will be filmed, what inner experiences will be explored, and what the general guidelines and framework will be.

Just like Disney decides what rides and attractions will be offered at its various theme parks, we all decide, as a group, what "rides," experiences, and games we'll play in our Earth amusement park.

The interesting thing is that as a group, we decide to change what we explore or how we explore it from time to time. Since we're in the middle of one of those changes right now, I felt it was important to make this seventh and final step a discussion of why this time in history is so special, how it's impacting your life, what you can expect as you move forward, and how you can better manage the unseen forces in operation during this unique time in history.

You know how, as a child or even as an adult, you sometimes play a game, see a movie, eat a food, or learn a skill and you like it so much you do it over and over? You play the game every day. You see the movie five times. You eat the food all the time. You practice and practice the skill. You can't get enough.

Eventually though, if you do it enough, the zing, the mystery, and the excitement level drop and you start to get bored. Then you start looking in new directions for stimulation, entertainment, or learning.

It's useful to look at what's happening throughout the world right now in the same way. All over the world, for hundreds, even thousands of years, we've been filming total immersion movies with a common theme running through them. We've explored so many of the "What would happen if?" scenarios within those themes that just like the overplayed game, the overwatched movie, or the overeaten food, they are starting to lose their zing and we're starting to look in new directions for stimulation, entertainment, and learning.

This is the reason so many civilizations throughout history flourished for so long then suddenly disappeared, declined, or were conquered. The examples that come to mind are the American Indians and South American Incas. There are many, many more of course.

These groups of people exhausted the possibilities of the "What would happen if?" scenarios they were playing with and, as a group, they chose to end the experiment and move on to new experiences.

All over the world, there's evidence that we're going from an old way of being, an old way of exploring, an old set of rides and attractions at our amusement park to a new way of being, a new way of exploring, and a new set of rides and attractions.

It's as if Disney World were involved in a major construction project to add new rides and attractions, renovate old ones, and eliminate the ones that just aren't as interesting anymore. If you walk into a toy store, you'll see old faithfuls like Monopoly and new sophisticated electronic toys. It's the same at Disney World. There are the old faithful attractions and the new high-tech attractions.

It's the same with us and the realities we choose to explore. Some people are finishing their old experiments and starting to move in the new direction. Other people are already moving in the new direction. As a group, we're not totally in either the old way of being or the new way of being—we're in transition between the two.

New ads are going into the network from behind the scenes; they're being translated into different experiences in our outer worlds. As a result, we're having new experiences in our inner worlds, too. "The Transition" has certain characteristics and guiding factors I'd like to share with you. The first major characteristic is that

The unconscious is coming to conscious.

What was hidden is being exposed. What was behind the scenes or beneath the surface is coming into the open to be looked at. Your old programming that isn't serving you anymore, the ads you've been sending into the network, the ads you've been responding to, and the P.S.'s that have been attached to your ads are all coming up to be looked at.

Why? So you can find out who you *really* are versus who a country, a religion, a teacher, a parent, a mentor, or anyone else programmed you to think you *should be.*

Throughout your personal transition, things will happen to you. People will flow in and out of your life and do things, say things, exert influences on you, and impact you in unusual ways.

Strange things may happen that cause you to rethink everything about who you are and how you live. You'll probably see the same things happening to the people you're closest to—and other people you don't even know. Be prepared!

You may change careers, change relationships, or make huge changes in your lifestyle. You may suddenly feel very drawn toward doing things you never considered before. Maybe this is already happening to you and you know exactly what I mean.

This process started for me many years ago when I got involved with a woman we'll call Catherine. We fell in love, moved in together, bought property together, and planned to get married. Suddenly, everything changed and our relationship fell apart. We ultimately broke up, got involved in a lawsuit over the property we owned, and I went through the most difficult year and a half of my life.

It was as if my director sent an ad into the network that said, "Bob has a lot of old, unresolved emotional stuff. It's time to take a look at it and release it. I need someone to come into his life, push all his buttons, and keep pushing them until this takes place." And Catherine volunteered for the job.

Old anger, old beliefs, old pain, and old confusion came spewing out. Old wounds I never even knew I had—consciously—got ripped open and salt was thrown in them.

It was a painful, exhausting experience, but looking back, it was also one of the greatest gifts I've ever received. I'd go through it all again in a flash to receive the tremendous benefits I got from it.

As a result of what that experience set in motion, I discovered The Invisible Path to Success and spent a lot of years learning how to navigate it.

I changed careers and relationships. I moved three times. I simplified my life, going from a complicated, fast-paced, stressful, and expensive lifestyle to a simple, slow-paced, relaxed, and very inexpensive lifestyle.

I lost a lot of weight. My energy level shot up. My health improved. A lifelong struggle with pimples on my face finally ended. I released a ton of "old programming" that had been keeping me stressed out and unhappy, and I discovered what love, happiness, and fulfillment really look and feel like.

The changes I made were dramatic, and I will always be grateful to Catherine for her part in that transformation.

As a part of The Transition, the volume on the unconscious side of life is being turned up. Everything that was once hidden is being exposed—the "good" and the "bad." Before we move into the new way of being, we want to put the old way of being to rest. Everyone, all over the world, wants to know what happened, why it happened, and what can be learned from it.

That's why so many people are teaching how to make relationships work, how the brain works, how to do everything better. Lots of "secrets" are being revealed for the first time about how life really works and how to be more effective at living it—including this book. That's also why you're seeing so many interesting, dramatic, confusing, and even shocking things coming out in the media these days.

There was a time when no one knew what was going on in other parts of the world. There was no television, no radio, no newspapers, no Internet. The world was a much bigger, more separated place. Now everyone is seeing and finding out about everything (specifically, what happened in all the "What would happen if?" scenarios we played out during the last phase of total immersion movie making).

This is also why so many people (maybe even you) are experiencing such personal challenges and tough, confusing times right now. The purpose is to help you understand what's been driving you, what's been going on inside you, and what's been causing you pain. It's helping you understand what's been going on beneath the surface and behind the scenes so you can cut through all the accumulated layers of "stuff" to find out who you really are (and who you are not) and to bring your entire life—your career, relationships, lifestyle, everything—into alignment with the real you.

The old way of being was designed so you didn't need to be aware of the behind-the-scenes, unconscious details. It was designed to run on autopilot beneath your awareness. Now that's changing. Now it's important to more *consciously* see, understand, and manage things in your life.

The second major characteristic of the Transition is that

All your energy is being pulled into the present from the future and the past.

In the old way of being, you'd set a goal of something you wanted in the future. Then everything in the present would be molded, shaped, altered, and sometimes *sacrificed* to get you there. The present was considered secondary to the future. Most of your life was driven by the future.

As an example, some time ago, my brother was dating a lot. Instead of just being in the moment, enjoying a woman's company, and not worrying about the future, whenever he met a woman, he'd instantly flash into the future and ask, "Could I see this woman as my wife? Is she *the one?*" I used to do the same thing, but when you do that, you leave the present moment and move into the future. Doing this creates a lot of tension and stress. It takes a lot of potential enjoyment out of the present moment because you're not there to enjoy it. And sometimes, when you try to project into the future to answer questions like "Is this woman *the one?*" at such an early date, you answer "no" when it's too soon to know and may end what might have been a nice experience no matter where it led.

When I stopped doing that, when I relaxed and just enjoyed the time I spent with women without caring about where I thought it might lead, I found my wife, Cecily, after just a few months!

I'll give you another example. I used to say, "I'll do 'X' (and you could fill in the "X" with anything I loved to do, like take a vacation, go out dancing, read a good novel, etc.) as soon as I finish this project or meet this deadline."

But there was always another project and another deadline, and I never got around to doing the things I loved to do. I've set up my life now so there are very few deadlines or demanding projects, so I'm usually free enough to ask myself what I really want to do in any given moment. I also give myself permission to say "no" to my wife, friends, or associates who ask me to do something I really don't want to do.

Your *past* also shapes a lot of your present. There's all the painful memories; the old "What does this mean?" and "How should I respond?" programming, the fears and worries that the past will repeat itself, and the old "neurotic patterns" that pull your energy and attention from the present moment back into the past.

When I was younger, because of some painful experiences, I shied away from new relationships, was extremely guarded, and didn't open up to many people. Why? Because I'd been so hurt and was afraid I'd get hurt again, I protected myself. Instead of being in the moment, just being there and seeing what really happened, I allowed myself to be pulled back into the past—once again sacrificing the present moment.

Mathematician and philosopher Pascal once said:

> *Let each man examine his thoughts, and he will find them all occupied with the past and the future. We scarcely ever think of the present, and if we think of it, it is only to take light from it to arrange the future. . . So we never live, but we hope to live; and, as we are always preparing to be happy, it is inevitable we should never be so.*

In my darkest and unhappiest days, I noticed that most of the time when I was stressed out, worried, or unhappy, I was in the past or the future—not in the moment. I also noticed that if I brought my attention back to the present, the pain, the stress, the worry, and the unhappiness disappeared almost immediately. Maybe the same will be true for you.

This "being in the moment" idea may not be new to you since it has been talked about in the "spiritual" literature for many years. What's different now is that instead of it just being a recommendation, the behind-the-scenes movie-making machinery is actively supporting you in really doing it!

What The Transition is taking you toward—where you're headed—is to know who you are (and who you are *not*), what you really want (and what you really *don't* want), and then let the present moment drive everything in your life.

We're moving into an environment where you'll passionately live in the present without an attachment to specific results or things looking a certain way. Where we're headed, you'll do what you do because you want to, not because you're afraid the past will repeat itself. You'll do things right now because you want to do them right now, not because doing them might give you something later or because you made the commitment a while ago and now you have to keep it.

I used to work with a well-known personal growth trainer whose life was booked up a year in advance. He was always committed to doing things before he had the chance to see if he really wanted to do them, if he'd really enjoy doing them, or if he'd rather do something else. I can't live like that anymore, although I did once.

Sometimes Cecily asks me in the morning what I want to do that evening. Sometimes she asks me on Wednesday what I'd like to do the following Sunday afternoon when she knows we're free. I tell her I don't know, that I'll make the decision then—when I know who I am and what I'll feel like doing at *that* moment.

Now obviously, sometimes you do plan things because it's not always possible to be totally spontaneous all the time. Other people you care about are often involved, and you can certainly get carried away with this being-in-the-moment idea, but you can start by taking a few baby steps before you crawl, walk, and then finally run down the road.

I'm not saying this because it's popular, it sounds cool, or because it makes sense. I'm saying it because if you really look at it, there's no other intelligent choice. Who you are, especially during this incredible Transition, is constantly changing, and there's just no way you can make decisions about your future now, way in advance, when you don't know who you'll be or what your life will be like when you arrive there. Think about it.

Moving through the Transition may be extremely difficult, provocative, or painful for you, as it was for me. It may be relatively easy, as it's been for my wife. Either way, the reward at the end of the tunnel will be tremendous, as you'll become so clear, become so focused, and bring your whole life—your career, your relationships, your lifestyle, everything—into alignment with who you really are and how you really want to live.

The Transition is a process I see everyone on the planet going through. You'll move through it at your own pace and in your own way. You'll be guided by your director every step of the way. There's no hurry, no deadline, and no timer running.

The unseen parts of your life, the invisible influences, and the programming that no longer serves you, will all be brought to the surface. You will look at them and make changes. You will find out who you really are, what you really want to do, and how you really want to live—no matter how easy or tough the process is.

Bottom line? You'll arrive at "the neutral point," where you'll say to yourself:

I'm in the moment. I know who
I am. Now, what do I want to do?

Then you'll do it—feeling free to change your mind and do something else whenever you choose to, including with relationshiops and careers. So what's the seventh step?

Sail with the winds of change.

A big wind is blowing. Put up your sails and allow it to fuel your journey to the neutral point, where you'll rediscover who you really are, and start a new way of living where your life explodes freely and fully out of the real you in the present moment.

Part Two

How to Navigate
The Invisible Path to Success

Chapter Eight

You've now taken all seven steps and reached what I call the "on-ramp" to The Invisible Path to Success. It's time to move a bit farther, step onto the path itself, and take it where you want to go. Let's start with a quick review of what you've discovered so far.

By taking the first step, you discovered there's often little value in intellectually debating right or wrong, true or false, accurate or inaccurate, or in making intellectual judgments on the validity of things without first testing them to see if they work *for you.*

You learned that the views I'm sharing here, like the views anyone shares anywhere, are only opinions that could be wrong, no matter what evidence is presented, how right it seems, or how powerful or successful the person with the opinion appears to be.

It was suggested that to be successful in navigating The Invisible Path to Success, it's useful to open your mind, let go of opinions, right and wrong, true and false, and base your strategies for living on what works *for you.*

By taking the second step, you learned that it can be very useful to look at your life as if it were a three-dimensional, total immersion movie experience, the sole purpose of which is to explore the *inner* experiences—thoughts, feelings, learning—that interest you.

You discovered that another part of you, an older, wiser part of you that's looking at your life from a broader perspective, is the director of your movie and is guiding every aspect of your life from behind the scenes to make sure you have the total immersion experience you came here for.

You learned it's useful to look at others on the planet, particularly the people who have an impact on your life, as actors or actresses playing a role. If they impact your life directly, they're playing the role you asked them to play in your movie, and they're following your script or the instructions you or your director gave them through the unconscious communications network.

By taking the third step, you learned that your life, while it appears complicated, is really only about two things: inner experience (what you think, what you feel, what you learn) and outer experience (what happens to you in the world you perceive through your five senses).

You learned that your inner experiences are shaped by the way you *unconsciously* answer the following questions "What does this mean?" and "How should I respond?" in response to what happens to you.

You discovered that the way you answer these questions (and decide what to think, feel, and do in response) is heavily influenced by your past experiences, education, conditioning, and programming, and that the time has come for you to turn off the cruise control and take back conscious control over this autopilot process when the results no longer serve you or help you create what you really want.

You also discovered that your programming was not an accident or the result of random forces, but the result of careful planning, monitoring, management, and guidance from behind the scenes by the director part of you.

By taking the fourth step, you learned that, on an unconscious level, every living thing on the planet is connected through a gigantic communications network that's much larger, more powerful, and easier to use than the Internet (and you don't need a computer).

You learned that everyone and everything in your life right now are the results of either an ad you sent into the network, an ad your director sent into the network, or an ad your director responded to on your behalf.

You learned there are no accidents and everything and everyone in your life are there by agreement and choice, and everyone—especially you—benefits from the interaction.

In step five, you learned that your analytical skills, while incredibly powerful, are still limited. You discovered you can often produce better results (or the same results with less effort) if you tap into the additional resources available through your director, crew, and the unconscious network.

You discovered that everybody's director communicates with them in different ways—sometimes through thoughts, sometimes through feelings, sometimes through dreams, meditation, books, or people you feel drawn to, etc. The important thing for you to do is learn to recognize the ways your director chooses to communicate with you.

In step six, you discovered what happens when you ask for things; whether you ask by using personal development techniques or as a result of your thoughts, beliefs, feelings, fears, attitudes, intentions, and expectations.

You learned that while you have unlimited power in theory, you choose to limit yourself when you commit to a specific exploration or adventure; as a result, you do not have unlimited power in practice. You learned that you always get a vote, but you don't always win the election. You discovered that your director often sends ads into the network or responds to other people's ads—whether you asked or not—on your behalf.

You also discovered that whenever you ask for something, your director decides if you'll receive it, what it will look like, and when it will show up—based on the purpose and goal of the current scene or set of scenes, and the bottom-line goal for your total immersion movie experience.

Finally, in step seven, you learned that there's a Transition taking place at this point in history. We're moving from an old way of being to a new way of being. You learned that as a group, we've exhausted the potentials of the "What would happen if?" scenarios we've been exploring and we're moving on to a new set of themes that will be explored in new ways.

You found out about the two primary factors driving this exciting Transition:

1. The unconscious is coming to conscious.
2. All your energy is being pulled into the present from the future and the past.

You discovered that people and events will be coming into your life (or are there already) and impacting you in specific ways. These people and events will enable you to cut through the layers of programming, habit, and conditioning, and help you to remember who you really are. They'll also help you find out what you really want; and bring your whole life—your career, your relationships, your lifestyle—into alignment with the real you.

You discovered that this process or Transition might be easy or tough for you, but whichever it is, the results and rewards will be well worth any pain you might experience.

You discovered that as you move through your own personal Transition, you'll eventually reach "the neutral point," where you'll begin a new approach to living, where you decide, day-by-day and moment-by-moment, what you want to do based on who you are and what you want to do *in that specific moment.*

I promised that I'd help you understand and manage the *unseen* forces shaping your life. By now it should be clear that there are actually four unseen forces at work:

1. The presence of your director, who filters your requests, makes requests on your behalf, and guides everything from behind the scenes so you get the total immersion experience you came for.
2. Your experiences being shaped by what you *really* want and the bottom-line purpose of your movie—rather than what you consciously *think* you want in any given scene.
3. The "What does this mean?" and "How should I respond?" machine that operates on autopilot to shape or determine what you think, feel, and do.
4. The unconscious communications network that you and your director use to get the actors, actresses, and crew together to tell them what to do, how to do it, and when to do it within your total immersion movie experience.

You're now ready to learn how to manage these unseen forces—to start actually navigating The Invisible Path to Success using the following steps as a road map. To make it simple, Chapters 9–14 are divided into six categories:

1. How to ask for what you want.
2. What to do if you don't receive what you asked for.
3. General suggestions for navigating The Invisible Path to Success.
4. How to better manage emotions, stress, and tough times.

5. How to navigate The Invisible Path to Success in your relationships.
6. How to navigate The Invisible Path to Success in your career, business, and finances.

Before continuing, it's important to repeat that when it comes to living a successful life within the context of The Invisible Path to Success, there are no rules, no formulas, no generalizations, no techniques, approaches, or systems that work for everyone.

You're here exploring something different from me and everyone else on the planet. You've been programmed differently from me and everyone else on the planet. You're headed to a different long-term destination than me and everyone else on the planet. What works for me might work for you. What works for someone else might work for you. It might not. The ideas I'm about to share with you have worked for me and many other people. They might work for you too. They might not.

But even if they don't work for you or you don't feel motivated to use them, I hope they'll at least give you some good ideas and a good starting point as well as stimulate you to create your own personalized, customized, unique ways of doing things.

Chapter Nine

How to Ask for What You Want

There are lots of ways to ask for what you want. You can use traditional goal-setting techniques, where you write down in detail what you want and when you want it. That works for a lot of people.

You can use visualization, where you close your eyes, go into a very relaxed state, and see and feel yourself having what you want with as much emotion as possible. There are many tapes, books, and courses available with instructions for doing this.

You can use affirmations, self-hypnosis tapes, subliminal tapes, NLP-based tapes, and the other self-help resources that are readily available through stores and catalogs.

It doesn't really matter what you do as long as you enjoy the process and remember that you're only asking your director for something you think you want, or attempting to reprogram your "What does this mean?" and "What should I do?" machine.

Although I use the techniques just mentioned from time to time, I generally do something a little different that works well for me. I use what I call my "wizard box." The idea is to have a box of some kind that you use to hold your requests or the symbolic representations of things you want to create in your life.

I've always loved the concept of wizards and magic. I collect wizards in all shapes, sizes, and forms. One day I saw a huge wizard cookie jar my wife later got for me as a gift. I now use that wizard box when I ask for things.

When there's something I want, I write it down very specifically and clearly on a sheet of paper (using the guidelines I'll be sharing in a minute). Then I put it in my wizard box with a lot of positive emotion and expectancy.

You can do all kinds of fun things with a "request box" like that. Say you want to be a writer. You can cut out pictures of successful writers who have the kind of career you'd like to have and put them in your box. You can put their book covers into the box. When you put these kinds of things in your box, it's like saying, "Hey director, this is something I want."

If you want a new car, cut out a picture of the car and put it in the box. If you see a picture of something in the newspaper and say, "I'd like that," put the picture in your box as a symbolic representation and request.

I know this sounds simple, but it really works for me. If you like the idea of a request box, it could be anything. It could be a wizard, if you like that idea. It could be something you make or buy. It could be anything, as long as it feels good to you and it makes you feel excited and powerful.

Another technique I've used is to create what is called a "focus wheel." I learned about this from my friend Abraham. Take a blank sheet of paper and draw a circle in the middle. Inside that circle write what you want.

Then, outside the circle, all around it, write the reasons why you want that thing and why you think you should have it; then draw a line that goes from your reasons into the circle. Then you can put the sheet in your request box.

Here's an example of what a focus wheel looks like.

How to Navigate the Path

You can actually write classified ads asking for what you want and put them into your request box, or do something else with them.

I know a woman who wrote a classified ad asking for something she wanted. Then she actually took it to the local newspaper and ran it. She didn't put a phone number in it; she just felt that running it made a statement to the Universe that was very powerful to her. By the way, she did receive what she asked for!

Use your imagination. Find a way of asking that's unique to you and that makes the process fun and exciting for you.

Whether you use my approach or something entirely different, there are a few guidelines I follow and you may want to follow too.

GUIDELINE NO. 1

Ask for everything

Always ask—especially when you're just starting to navigate The Invisible Path to Success. Ask for even the smallest things. Before you do anything (attend a business meeting, go on a date, make a sales call, begin a seminar, ask someone for a favor, go to sleep, etc.) always make your desires, wishes, and intentions clear, and ask for what you want in the situation.

Your director manages all the details and makes sure everything is in alignment with your movie, but you're still meant to be an active participant in it. You're meant to have experiences, react to them, ask for things, share what you want and don't want, and give your director feedback on what's going on in your inner experience. It's an important part of the process.

Whenever you ask, you are making sure your director knows it's something you *really* want—versus a passing thought or fleeting desire. It's an opportunity for an ad to go into the network and for you to receive a positive response to it.

If you don't ask, your ad can't go into the network and there's no way anyone can respond positively to you (unless it's something your director was working on anyway).

Let me give you a few minor and major examples of how powerful this process can be for you.

When I go on a trip and check my luggage at the counter or curbside, I always ask for my luggage to arrive in perfect shape and for it to be one of the first few bags to come off the baggage claim carousel.

Nine times out of ten, when I remember to ask (and sometimes I forget), it happens exactly as I ask. If I don't ask and my director doesn't intercede, who knows what will happen, when the luggage will come off the carousel, or what shape it will be in.

I once had a mole removed. A big piece of skin around the mole was taken off as well and it left a big wound that had to be stitched up. I put one of my sheets into my wizard box asking that it heal perfectly and quickly.

A while ago, Cecily and I got a new puppy we named Mollie. It was our second dog. Potty training Peri, our first dog, was a total nightmare and took forever. We didn't want to go through that again, so this time we sent an ad into the network saying we would honor and respect whatever Mollie wanted, but from our perspective we wanted her potty training to be easy and go quickly. That's exactly what happened.

If you're confused or need help with something, send an ad into the network asking for clarity or the kind of guidance you want.

This is what I love so much about The Invisible Path to Success. No matter what you want or need, ask for it. If it's part of your movie, you'll get it. If it's not part of your movie, you'll get something even better.

Asking can also stop old programming or your "What does this mean?" and "How should I respond?" machine from creating ads or P.S.'s and sending them into the network without your wanting them to.

I'll give you a simple example, but know that it happens with even the biggest things. I used to have a pattern of always getting in the slowest lane at the grocery checkout area. It was uncanny. I'd always look for the line I thought would move the fastest, and time after time I'd be drawn to the line that moved the slowest. I could never figure out why.

Then one day I started consciously asking to be guided to the lane that would move the fastest. I stopped letting an unconscious autopilot ad run my life. And you know what? It doesn't happen anymore. I changed the programming. I interrupted the pattern. A new ad went to my assistants and into the network, and my results changed.

The same thing happened to me with finances, relationships, and other old patterns that used to drive me.

When my wife opened her yoga studio, we mailed and dropped off flyers all over the city announcing her grand opening. There was no way Cecily and I could make sure the flyers got into the hands of the right people. We didn't know who the right people were in most cases, especially when we mailed the flyers to businesses with lots of people in them. There was also no way we could make sure the right people would see our flyers on the tables or bulletin boards where we left them.

So we sent an ad into the network asking for help in linking the right people with our flyers. We asked that the people who could really benefit from yoga, the people who would be most likely to become regular students, would find their way to our flyers and come to the grand opening. We wrote up one of our little sheets and put it in the wizard box.

The result? A packed room at the grand opening, lots of enrollments, and a good start for the school.

GUIDELINE NO. 2
Create instead of react

Oftentimes, instead of creating or asking for what we want, we simply react to what's happening to us. Something happens, we react, and we start focusing on our reaction instead of focusing on what we want.

For example, you're about to go on a date and you focus on all the bad things that might happen. You have a big presentation to make and worry about blowing it. Or an unexpected expense crosses your path and you suddenly start worrying about money. On and on.

If you find yourself afraid, worried, or nervous about something, instead of focusing on it, which *can* translate into an ad that goes into the network or a P.S. that gets attached to an ad, immediately send an ad into the network asking for what you want instead.

This is where the focus wheel technique can really come in handy. Instead of worrying about a date going badly, immediately send an ad into the network or do a focus wheel asking for what you want to happen on the date.

Instead of worrying about blowing your presentation at an important meeting, immediately send an ad into the network or do a focus wheel asking for the result you think you want. Instead of worrying about money when an unexpected expense crosses your path, send an ad into the network or do a focus wheel on what you want to happen in your financial life.

Since you only get a vote but you don't always win the election, you may not receive what you ask for, but asking and stopping a contradictory ad or a limiting P.S. from going into the network can increase the odds you will receive it—*if it's part of your movie.*

GUIDELINE NO. 3

Remember how limited your perspective is

When asking for what you want, start out by saying, feeling, or understanding that from the limited perspective of your conscious mind, what you're asking for is only what you think you want. It may not be what you really want. It may not even be the best thing for you, even if you're sure it is.

It's important to start by admitting, to yourself and the Universe, how little you see and know about your movie, what you're asking for, etc. My friend Ava suggested a little affirmation I often use after asking for something. It goes like this:

> *From the limited perspective of my conscious mind, this is what I think I want, and I ask that you give me this or something even better.*

Sometimes when I say this, people ask me, "Won't asking with that thought or feeling create a P.S. that weakens my request or lessens the chance I'll receive what I'm asking for?" From my experience, that doesn't happen. Your director knows what you're doing and knows you're only speaking the truth as you know it.

Plus, taking this approach can work wonders for the stress, frustration, and anger that sometimes come when you ask for things and don't get them, don't get them as fast as you want them, or they don't look quite how you pictured.

GUIDELINE NO. 4
Ask as if you're talking directly to your director

As you're writing, visualizing, using affirmations, meditating, or whatever you do, imagine there's an actual being with you listening and paying attention. Feel her presence.

GUIDELINE NO. 5

*Define your "surface goal" and the inner
experience beneath it that you really want*

Whenever you ask for something, there is always a "surface goal" as well as the inner experience beneath it that you really want. For example, if you ask for a man or woman to come into your life for a new relationship, the relationship is the surface goal. But there's an *inner experience* beneath it that's more important to you. It might be feeling love, excitement, or companionship. It could be anything.

Whenever you ask for something, it's possible to achieve your surface goal and *not* get the inner experience beneath it that you really want. For example, suppose your surface goal is wanting a new relationship and the inner experience beneath it (what you really want) is the feeling of being loved.

Have you ever been in a relationship where you didn't feel loved? I sure have. If you haven't, is it possible to be in a relationship and not feel loved even though you want it? I think you'd agree it's possible.

The surface goal is only a *possible* route to the inner experience you want. It may or may not actually produce it.

It's important to always ask for the surface goal *and* the inner experience you really want. That way, you increase the odds you'll create what you really want. Does that make sense?

I'll give you another example related to my wife's yoga studio. Cecily's surface goal was to share "Bikram yoga" with as many people as possible, make friends in the community, and create a nice income for herself. The inner experience she really wanted was the joy she gets from teaching yoga. She also wants the feeling of knowing she's helping other people. She wants to feel that she's in charge—that she's running the school (not that the school is running her life). As a result, she wants it to suit her lifestyle in terms of how many hours a week she teaches, what time the classes are, how many people are in each class, etc.

If Cecily just sent an ad into the network asking to share yoga, make friends, and create a nice income for herself, she might get it, but she might get it and be stressed out, not enjoy the teaching, not feel like she's making a contribution, and not have an enjoyable lifestyle.

If she asked for the inner feelings she wanted, but she didn't ask for sharing yoga with as many people as possible, making friends, and having the nice income, she wouldn't be getting what she really wanted either.

When she asks for everything she wants—her surface goal and the inner experience beneath—she increases the odds she'll get it. It's the same for you and me and everyone else.

GUIDELINE NO. 6
Remember that your ads are always taken literally

Always remember that when looking at your ads, requests and P.S.'s, your director and the Universe will take things literally. There's no second-guessing, no reading between the lines, no interpretation or guesswork.

If your ad isn't clearly asking for something, as in the case of the young woman dreaming of going to China, no one will respond. If there's a P.S. in your ad, the P.S. will be taken literally and could undercut or "sabotage" your ad.

GUIDELINE NO. 7

Leave your ads and requests open-ended

Since your ads will be taken literally by your director, assistants, and the Universe, it's important to make sure you don't put any artificial limitations or ceilings on your request.

If you have artificial limiters in your ad, like the young man who was asking for a $2,000-a-month job although he really wanted something better, you'll get a limited response.

I always add "or more," "or sooner," "or better" to my wording to leave it open-ended for the Universe and my director.

I'll give you an example of how powerful this can be. A few years ago I sold my Nordic Track ski machine and bought a very expensive Nordic Track machine that had a skier, treadmill, and stair stepper all together in one unit. It cost me $1,500.

I used it for a while and didn't really like it. It was noisier than my other Nordic Track. I found I never used the stepper, and some of the features I thought would be really great weren't that great after all.

I decided to sell the new Nordic Track and reorder the one I used to have. So I put a classified ad in the newspaper offering it for sale at $1,000. I also sent an ad into the unconscious network asking that I receive my asking price *or more* for the unit.

I got some nibbles from the newspaper ad, but didn't sell it. Then the machine started to malfunction. So I called Nordic Track and asked what I should do. They told me they'd discontinued the machine, they couldn't fix it for me, and they'd send a truck to pick it up and give me a full refund. That meant I'd receive $1,500 for the unit—$500 more than I would have gotten in the best-case scenario from my newspaper ad.

I know that if I hadn't put "or more" into my unconscious ad, that would never have happened. Why? Because the possibility of getting a full refund from Nordic Track never crossed my mind and never would have crossed my mind as a way to create what I really wanted—which was to receive as much money as possible when I sold the unit.

Although that possibility never occurred to me, it obviously occurred to my director! By leaving the door open, I allowed my director to create something even better for me. Had my unconscious ad been to receive my asking price of $1,000, my director and the Universe would have complied, and I would be $500 poorer today.

Leaving things open-ended can be subtle, but so powerful!

GUIDELINE NO. 8

Be only as specific as is appropriate to the situation

Most self-help systems tell you to be very specific when setting goals or asking for things you want. I disagree. Sometimes it's best to be very specific when you ask for things and at other times it's best to be very general and let your director give your request a specific shape. Let me give you some examples.

When Cecily and I had our grand opening for the yoga studio, we had 75 open places for a series of free classes we were offering. In our flyers, we asked people to call for reservations since we knew we'd fill the slots.

We wanted to send an ad into the network to support our surface world marketing efforts. We could have asked for 75 reservations, but just because someone makes a reservation doesn't mean they'll actually show up—especially when it's free. We could have asked for 75 people to actually show up, but they might not have been the "right" 75 people—people who would become regular students, which is what we really wanted.

So we sent an ad into the network asking to fill the grand opening classes with people who were likely to become regular students or who knew people who were likely to become regular students.

Believe it or not, since Cecily didn't want to waste her time or energy on people who didn't fit this profile, we also asked that anyone who might come across our flyer, or hear about the grand opening but did not fit our profile, be discouraged from coming.

In this case, we were very specific because we knew what we really wanted. And we did leave the ad open-ended so the Universe could give us something even better.

But there are times when it's better not to be so specific—when asking for a new relationship, for example. Some people tell you that to bring that perfect person into your life, you should write everything down in incredible detail—from hair color to body shape, from job to personality.

Given how little you know about who you really are, what you really want, what kind of person would really make you happy, what your movie is about, etc., what you think is the best mate for you may not be accurate.

It may be accurate, but it's not likely. And if you're too specific (since the Universe takes everything literally), you can limit the Universe in its ability to respond to you.

My brother used to resist dating women who were shorter than five feet four inches. He also resisted dating women who were too much younger than he was.

While I have no idea what his movie is about or what's right for him, from my perspective he was limiting himself with those beliefs. What if the perfect woman for him, a woman he could really be happy with for the rest of his life, was one inch shorter than his limit or one year younger? The way his ads were going into the network and the way the Universe takes everything literally, he might have missed out on a terrific opportunity depending on what his movie was all about. He has since come to the same conclusion.

The same is often true with money and career. Say you want a monthly income of $10,000. Maybe it would be best to ask for $10,000 a month from doing a specific thing you like to do, like selling computers, writing books, or being an attorney.

But maybe it would be better to ask for $10,000 a month coming in any way that aligns with who you really are, isn't too stressful, etc., and leave it open-ended.

Just like my experience with the Nordic Track refund, there are many possible places a monthly $10,000 income could come from—places you might never think of consciously.

Run an ad asking for what you want to do (with regard to your interest in selling, writing, or being an attorney), but make it separate from the money. It's the same thing with many of the other things you think you want.

Are you starting to see some of the exciting possibilities that navigating The Invisible Path to Success holds for you?

Sometimes it's better, even if you choose to be specific, to be specific but leave the door open by saying something like, "My preference would be 'x,' but if there's something better for me, so be it. I'm open to that."

Sometimes it's just better to let your director shape the granting of your requests. Your director knows what your movie is about, what this set of scenes is about, and what the upcoming scenes are going to be about. Your director has access to the network to get anything done or any question answered. Let her give it shape when you ask.

GUIDELINE NO. 9
Take your time when writing your ads

You're working with very powerful forces here and although you might be anxious to bring certain things into your life or change certain things you're not happy with, I recommend you take your time writing your ads and sending them into the network. There's no hurry.

GUIDELINE NO. 10
After you ask, let go, trust, and flow

After you ask, however you ask, let go, trust your director, and flow with what you feel *strongly* motivated to do. Resist the temptation of getting attached to, or having an emotional investment in, your request being granted in a certain way or within a certain time frame.

If you become too attached to or emotionally invested in a particular outcome, you set yourself up for pain or disappointment. It might be part of your movie to experience that pain and disappointment, but it might also be unnecessary.

An interview I saw with Olympic swimmer Matt Biondi is a good example. In one Olympics, everyone expected him to win a gold medal in every single event he was in. When Matt didn't win a gold medal in his first event, people were upset. They called him a big disappointment, a failure—all because what happened didn't match their expectations. Since they were so emotionally invested in a certain outcome, it was very painful to them when it didn't happen.

Matt had no such goal for himself. His goal was to go to the Olympics, do the best he possibly could, and accept the outcome. He ended up doing very well, but from what I saw, he was *not* emotionally invested in a specific outcome. Depending on what your movie is about, not being emotionally invested in or attached to specific outcomes better prepares you to deal with life's ups and downs. It gives you more flexibility and more options. It can also prevent unwanted P.S.'s from "sneaking" into your ads.

It may be part of your movie to be very invested in specific outcomes and to experience pain if you don't experience them. But if it's not part of your movie, you can drop a lot of stress out of your life by not being invested and being able to go with the flow a bit more.

Say you ask for something, your director approves your ad, sends it into the network, deals with the responses, makes agreements on your behalf, and you're going to receive what you asked for. What might happen in your life? You might get an idea, feel motivated to do something, go somewhere, talk to someone, buy a book, or attend a seminar. The key is to be open, to do what you feel *strongly* motivated to do and to do it without overanalyzing. Why? Because with the limitations of your analytical skills, you don't necessarily know what the response to your ad or request *should* look like.

Your ad can be responded to in any way, at any time, under any circumstances. You don't know when or how the moment will be, so approach your life with excitement and anticipation.

Ask yourself all the time, "Is this the moment I'm going to receive what I want—or something even better? Is what

I want at the next party, around the next corner?" Get excited. Responses to your ads can come from anywhere at any time.

Some people recommend visualizing what you want every day until it shows up. Or rereading and rewriting your goals every day. Or repeating affirmations daily or putting them on your mirror or steering wheel until you get what you want.

That kind of repetition works for some people, particularly as a reprogramming technique, but it doesn't work for everyone. If you feel motivated to use such a repetitive approach, use it and see if it works for you. If you don't feel motivated to use a repetitive technique, ask once; then let it go. Trust that your director is going to take care of you and flow with what you feel strongly motivated to do. I only ask once unless something happens that causes me to change the way I'm asking or what I'm asking for.

No matter what happens, always remember that the Universe is 100 percent for you, 0 percent against you, and you always get what you asked for—or something even better!

What's the bottom line when it comes to asking for what you want? Find a technique or approach that feels good to you and use it. You need never again settle for "generic" or "hit or miss" strategies for getting what you really want in life. Decide what you think you want. Consciously send ads into the network asking for your own *customized* solutions and answers. Trust that you'll get what you asked for—or something even better. Flow with what you feel *strongly* motivated to do.

Chapter Ten

What to Do if You Don't Receive What You Asked For

If you ask for something in your life and you don't receive it, there are only a few possible explanations.

1. Your request wasn't clear. Remember the woman who wanted to raise $5,000 to go to China to teach kids English, find a nice place to live, and make friends, but whose ad was so murky it wasn't actually asking for anything clearly.
2. A P.S., allowed by your director, got in the way. We often counter or immediately cancel our requests because a contradictory P.S. finds its way into our ads.
3. You're being impatient. It's coming, but the timing isn't right yet.
4. What you asked for is not in alignment with your movie or this set of scenes and you're not going to get it.
5. You didn't get your surface goal but you did get the inner experience beneath it that you really wanted. You succeeded. You just didn't realize it.

If your request wasn't clear or a P.S. interfered, you can do something to change your request and you might still get it.

If you're going to get what you asked for but the timing isn't right yet, there's nothing you can do but wait.

If what you asked for isn't in alignment with your movie in general or the current set of scenes in specific, you're not going to get it—no matter how much you try, how many techniques you use, how many books you read, how many seminars you attend, or how many experts and psychics you consult.

In some cases, it's best to just let go of your request and go on to other things or rethink what you really want. Remember, your life is not necessarily about what you think you want *consciously* in any given moment. It's about the overall *inner experiences* you want to explore over your entire lifetime.

This is so important because continuing to push when you don't get what you asked for can cause so much pain. I can't tell you how much frustration I experienced, how much I beat myself up, and how many moments of anger, desperation, and confusion I had because I kept pushing and trying to force something to happen when I didn't get what I asked for.

On many occasions, after I pushed and pushed and pushed and wouldn't give up, my director finally said, "Okay, I'll give it to you just so you can see you don't really want it," and he gave it to me so I'd understand this important point.

When I finally did get the things I'd been pushing for, they didn't give me what I'd hoped for at all. It wasn't even close most of the time.

If you didn't get what you asked for, here are some steps you can follow:

1. Give yourself a break.

Resist any temptation to beat yourself up or think you did something wrong. You're just fine. You did everything right, and there are a variety of possibilities as to why you didn't get what you asked for. Be prepared and willing to explore those possibilities, but resist the temptation to think you did something "wrong."

2. Ask for help with P.S.'s.

If you suspect a P.S. stopped your request from being granted or you want to eliminate it as a possibility, send an ad into the network asking for help in uncovering and removing any P.S.'s that might have impacted your request.

You can also ask your director to help you through your dreams, when you meditate, or through whatever other communication method you prefer.

If it's part of your movie to uncover or change a P.S., it will happen. If it's not, it won't—or it won't happen at the exact moment you think you want it.

In my life, some of the deepest and most powerful P.S.'s took a long time to be uncovered and changed. In many cases, even though I was desperate to uncover and erase P.S.'s I knew were hurting me, it didn't happen because there was benefit to me in allowing them to impact me a while longer. When the timing was finally right, the P.S. surfaced and disappeared quickly and easily. The same may be true for you.

3. Check to see if you achieved your inner-experience goal.

Ask yourself, "If I didn't get the surface goal, did I get some or all of the inner experience beneath it that I really wanted?"

There was a time in my life when my surface goal was to bring more money into my life, but what I really wanted was to be free of the constant worry I had about not having enough money.

I got more money in response to my ad, but the stress and worry about money didn't go away, although I had a lot more of it.

In that case, I got my surface goal, but I didn't create what I really wanted, so I wasn't happy. Then I changed my ad, and asked for the inner experience of feeling good about money. It took a while, but I finally got the feeling and the relationship with money I really wanted. Then I was happy because the feeling was much more important to me.

If you discover you didn't achieve your surface goal but you did create the inner experience beneath it, celebrate! You got what you really wanted. You can still work on getting the surface goal if you want to, but celebrate anyway because you got what was most important to you.

4. Make sure you were specific in asking for what you wanted.

It can be subtle, but you may not be specific enough or you may be complaining about the absence of something instead of asking for what you want.

When I was younger, I had a roll of extra fat on my waistline. For years I used a variety of techniques for losing weight. I did lose weight, sometimes a lot of weight, but the extra fat on my waist remained.

One day I realized I wasn't asking for what I wanted specifically enough. When I finally sent an ad into the network asking for help in *losing the extra fat on my waist,* it disappeared quickly.

Asking to lose weight and burn fat off the waist are similar, but in a Universe that takes things literally, they're also very different. If you ask to lose weight, you'll lose weight—if it's part of your movie. If you ask to burn extra fat off your waistline, you'll burn off extra fat off your waistline—if it's part of your movie.

Here's another example. For years my life was difficult and filled with stress. I complained about things being so difficult. I asked myself all the time, "Why can't things be easier?" But it never occurred to me to actually *ask* to achieve my goals, get what I want, and have the process be easy.

When I finally asked, things started getting easier and easier and they finally did become easy. It took a few years for everything to shift and fall into place just right, but things changed radically for me. Sometimes we just forget to ask!

5. Rethink your request.

Many times I sent ads into the network, didn't receive what I asked for, and later realized after some other things happened that I didn't really want what I was asking for after all. Or I realized I wanted it, but I wanted it to be a little different from my first request. Or I didn't receive what I asked for, but I got something even better that I'd never even thought about before.

I'll give you another example from our experience opening the yoga studio. Cecily and I started looking for a space to rent for the school. We had an idea of the size, shape, and location we wanted.

We found three spaces that looked like they'd meet our needs. We started negotiating with the landlords and they were tough to deal with.

In each case, we got very close to signing deals for spaces that would have worked but weren't perfect (we would have had to spend a lot of our own money to renovate the interiors to make it work for us).

The deals fell through at the last minute for what we considered strange reasons. But each time it happened, we noticed we were getting more and more clear on what we wanted and what we *didn't* want.

We ultimately decided we wanted a smaller space in a different area, and we didn't want to have all the out-of-pocket, start-up expense. When we made that decision, a new and more powerful ad went into the network. A few days later, we finally found the absolutely perfect space with a wonderful landlord. The landlord not only gave us a great rate on the square footage, but he paid $13,000 out of his own pocket to do the renovations we needed done. It was amazing.

If you follow these five steps and still don't receive what you asked for—your surface goal or the inner experience beneath it—the only other thing I can recommend is that you send an ad into the network asking for clarity from your director and guidance on what to do next.

Say something like, "I asked for this thing. I didn't receive it. I'm confused about what to do next. Please guide me, give me a sign, give me some clarity. Is the answer no? Is it coming soon? Is there something I can do to change things? Is something better coming? etc."

If you meditate now or have another way of communicating with your director, have a chat with him and ask for clarity that way.

You get the idea.

Chapter Eleven

General Suggestions for Navigating
The Invisible Path to Success

Every day, all day long, you have to make decisions. Some decisions are small, others are big and important.

Before I discovered The Invisible Path to Success, I used to worry a lot about making mistakes when it came to the bigger decisions. I believed I had a certain destiny, something specific I came here to do, and if I went right instead of left at a fork in the road, I'd mess everything up and trash my destiny forever.

That might sound silly to you. It does to me looking back, but it's how I felt at the time. It caused me a lot of stress and worry and used to sort of "freeze" me for a while when I had a big decision to make.

If you take everything I've shared with you so far, a subtle but very important conclusion is

You can't make a mistake.

First of all, depending on what your movie is about, there might not be that many times when you're "meant" to go right instead of left, take this job instead of that one, do this instead of that.

But suppose you were meant to go right at a fork in the road and you went left instead. What would happen? Would you trash your whole destiny? No! Your director, with all the resources at her disposal, can easily guide you back onto the "right track" again.

What is the process you use to make decisions? Do you think about it for a while? Do you talk to other people, use your intuition, trust your gut, or just wing it?

Want to know something interesting? Your director can influence *all those things*. Your director can communicate with you through all the channels you use to make decisions.

He can plant seeds in your thoughts or feelings. He can bring people in or out of your life. He can influence whether you hook up with someone you want advice from or create any kind of experience he wants you to have.

He can also communicate with you through your dreams, meditations (if you do them), the words of other people, a book or tape he helps cross your path. The options are endless. Your job is to find out how he talks to you!

I'm sure you've experienced this or heard stories of people who need to find an answer or solve a problem. They think and think and think and get nothing. Then suddenly, while they're in the shower, shaving, or doing something totally unrelated, the answer pops out.

What's happening there? You asked for what you wanted. Your director started working on it for you. While you were waiting, she was scanning your memory banks, sending ads into the network, getting responses, and evaluating the options against your movie or current scene. Then, when she had the right answer for you, and you were ready to hear it, it popped out.

Many times I felt motivated to do things. I made a decision and started moving in a certain direction, but I kept getting blocked. People wouldn't return my calls. Things would get lost in the mail. There would be endless delays. Appointments would be canceled. People wouldn't do what they said they'd do. On and on.

When I bump into resistance like that now, I can usually see that there's a message in it for me and I step back, stop pushing, and start looking for that message. What usually happens next is that something even better crosses my path—sometimes almost immediately.

If you're unsure of which way to go at a decision-making point in your life, you can close your eyes, flash into the future in your imagination (or in a meditative state), see yourself experiencing all the possible options and see which one *feels* better, or *feels* more right or comfortable to you.

Be as smart as you can be. Be as cautious as you feel is appropriate to the situation. Use your analytical skills and mental powers. Use your intuition. Talk to other people, meditate, ask for help, however you do it. Then relax, make the decision, and do what you feel strongly motivated to do—even if it defies logic, even if it defies what the experts say or what other people tell you to do.

A lot of the world's greatest success stories came as a result of someone going against the grain or in the opposite direction of what the experts and the crowd said to do.

Then trust and flow, knowing your director will take care of you and your movie will end up taking you where you want to go. You no longer need to worry about finding your life purpose. You no longer need to wonder if you'll ever fulfill it or if you somehow messed it up. Your general purpose is to explore the inner experiences that interest you. Your specific purpose *will be fulfilled.* There's no way you can fail. Your director will see to it that you succeed—no matter what happens or what decisions you make.

Perhaps this idea that you can't make a mistake will give you the kind of stress relief I've found so valuable in my life.

People are very different from one another. They have different opinions, different ways of looking at things, different ways of reacting to things, and different ways of doing things. I used to look at what other people said and did, and I often realized it made no sense to me. I began to wonder how we could be so different from one another. I began to wonder,

- Do we all see the same things and interpret them differently?
- Do we actually see entirely different things?
- Is it both?

I concluded it's both.

Our directors guide certain experiences into our lives based on the scripts of our movies. As a result, the world you see day to day is very different from the world I see—and the world everyone else sees.

But it doesn't stop there. Since we've had such different experiences, our "What does this mean?" and "How should I respond?" machines will interpret things differently—even if we're seeing the same things.

So on two levels, everyone on the planet is experiencing completely different worlds on a day-to-day basis. That's why people disagree so much—because each of us "sees" and interprets things so differently.

I now salute the differences in people. I respect them. I celebrate them. Perhaps you can do the same thing.

It's why we're here—it's what makes life interesting.

Chapter Twelve

**How to Follow the Invisible Path to
Better Manage Emotions, Stress, and Tough Times**

In life we have *positive* emotions such as love, joy, happiness, and confidence. We also have *negative* emotions such as fear, guilt, and anger. We enjoy the positive emotions and tend to seek them out, but we struggle with the negative ones.

When talking about emotions as they relate to The Invisible Path to Success, it's important to remember that your total immersion movie is about having inner experiences. A huge part of your inner experience is emotion, and that means both positive *and* negative emotions.

It's helpful to understand that positive emotions aren't good and negative emotions aren't bad. They're just different experiences and you're here to explore both.

When we are happy or sad, it has meaning. Emotion is the spotlight that illuminates opportunities to experience purely, grow, evolve, or improve ourselves. Seeking ways to blot out variations in mood or feeling is equivalent to an airline pilot ignoring his navigational instruments.

Since it's such an important subject and far too complex to cover in this chapter alone, I've devoted an entire book in The Invisible Path series to the subject of understanding and managing *inner experience.* For now, however, let me share the following ideas with you.

Most of the emotions you experience in a given day are the result of how you're answering the questions "What does this mean?" and "How should I respond?" at the unconscious level. In other words, you feel the way you've *learned* to feel about things.

Sometimes it's best to just experience emotions (whether they're positive or negative), allow them to flow through you and fully express themselves, then let them go and get on with your life. At other times, it's valuable and important to change the way your questions are being answered so you can change how you feel as a result.

If you want guidance on how to actually do this or how to know when to do what, simply send an ad into the network asking to be guided to the people, ideas, resources, opportunities, and actions that can help you create the result you want.

When I really understood that I'm taken care of from behind the scenes, that my director monitors everything, manages everything, and makes sure that only what I really want to explore touches my life, I noticed that I started feeling a lot more positive emotions and a lot fewer negative emotions. The same thing could happen for you.

For example, Cecily and I live in Florida, which gets a lot of hurricanes during five to six months of the year. As you know, hurricanes put your life, health, and possessions at risk. We're smart about it. We're cautious. We stock up on food, water, flashlights, and batteries. We pay attention and would certainly evacuate if it ever came to that. But we don't have a lot of fear about the situation. Why? Because we trust that our directors will take care of us. We trust that if a dangerous hurricane were to ever hit here, we'd be guided to leave the area in advance or our movies would still proceed according to plan if we stayed—no matter what happened.

Sometimes, out of fear, we have a great need to know what's going to happen to us in advance. From my experience, knowing in advance isn't always part of your movie script, nor is it the best thing for you.

Have you ever seen the same movie or television show several times? I don't know about you, but if I see something multiple times, I might still enjoy it, but eventually I won't. Why? Because I know everything that's going to happen. The mystery is gone. A lot of the inner experience I enjoyed so much is gone or faded, and as a result, it isn't as rewarding.

When a movie is being filmed, the actors and actresses don't usually know how it will look or how it will all be pieced together in the final version you and I see on the big screen. They know bits and pieces, but they're usually surprised when they see the final version on the screen themselves. Because scenes are not always shot sequentially, they do their parts in an isolated way and then they see how it all comes out later. It's the same with your life and the movie in which you're the star!

If you want to know why something is happening to you, or at least explore the possibilities, look to what was set in motion in your inner experience or daily life for clues. It may not be part of your movie to know the answer, but if it is, that's where you'll find the clues.

It's the same if you want to know why something is happening to others. Look to what was set in motion in *their* inner experiences or daily lives as a result for clues.

I'll give you a very personal example of this and then a few public ones.

My cousin Rebekah once took a trip to a small town in Africa. She and her group were walking down a main street when a van came speeding into town, out of control. It hit both Rebekah and one of her friends who was next to her.

Rebekah's friend was killed instantly. Rebekah was badly hurt, with a broken pelvis, arm and leg, and bruises everywhere.

When I first heard about it, I felt terrible for her. I knew she was okay, but imagining her long road to recovery and all the pain made me wince inside.

Then I found myself asking, "I wonder why that experience was part of her movie?"

As I understand it, her friend was killed, she was badly injured, and no one else in her group was hurt at all. The difference between getting killed, getting badly hurt, and being untouched was a matter of a few feet.

From the perspective of The Invisible Path to Success, at the unconscious level, everyone's director knew about the van in enough time to do something about it. The director of the girl who got killed could have easily arranged for her to move a few feet out of the way. Rebekah's director could have easily gotten her to move a few feet out of the way. Or the director of the person driving the van could have easily sent the van somewhere else or caused it to brake or swerve away from the girls before hitting them.

From the perspective of The Invisible Path to Success, this was no accident. It was allowed by the directors of everyone involved. Why? Because it set something into motion in the movies of everyone involved that benefited them, either in the short or long term.

What was the benefit? I'll never know in the case of the van driver, the girl who was killed, or the other people in Rebekah's group. If I want to find some clues about why it happened to Rebekah, I'd watch to see what happened in her inner experience and what was set into motion as a result. That's what I'll be doing over time as the story continues to unfold.

And again, I may never know—*consciously*—why it happened or what the benefit was. Rebekah may never know—*consciously*—why it happened or what the benefit was.

What's important in situations like this is to switch from an attitude of viewing it as a terrible random accident to an attitude of looking at it as being created (or allowed) with intelligence and planning—with benefit for all concerned.

If you find this difficult to accept, I ask you again: Why is it so much easier to believe in randomness, accidents, tragedy, and victims than it is to believe in purpose, intelligence, choice, and benefit?

The front pages of recent newspapers included the following three stories:

1. The aftermath of the Princess Diana car crash.
2. Continued searches for debris and an explanation for why a TWA jet exploded in midair.
3. A case where someone abused a six-month-old child, but authorities don't know who was responsible.

If you want to know why these things happened (and again you may never know), investigate and see what these events set in motion for the people involved directly and indirectly. That's where you'll find your answers or at least some clues.

As another example, think of the O.J. Simpson trial. No matter what you think about O.J., the crime, or the verdict, a lot of things were set in motion in the lives of O.J., his kids, Nicole's family, the Goldman family, the attorneys, and many others.

A lot of international attention was focused on the subjects of spousal abuse, hero worship, the legal system, and race relations. Many seeds were planted in very fertile earth!

Similarly, there was much press coverage about safety problems of an airline called Valujet. A lot of people died in a crash and the airline was temporarily shut down. "Why, why, why?" My answer? Look at what was set in motion in the lives of the survivors of the people who died, the people related to the airline itself, and the people in the airline industry, etc., for clues.

This brings me to one of the most important points to be made in this book.

> *Nothing is allowed to come into your life*
> *and have an impact on you unless*
> *it's arranged or allowed by your director.*

There is no randomness; there are no accidents. While you're riding the roller coaster, does someone from the haunted house ride suddenly jump in, sit next to you in the middle of the ride, and interrupt your experience? No! They ride their ride and you ride yours. Everything is kept separate.

If you look around, you could be so frozen with fear you'd never do anything. The Valujet airline crash I just mentioned was supposedly caused by a damaged oxygen canister. That kind of "accident" can happen anywhere or anytime, and you'd never have advanced notice, much less be able to stop it.

If you think about how many murderers, thieves, rapists, and criminals there are who could get you, or you think about all the possibilities for car accidents, getting diseases, or getting hurt in sports, you'd go crazy with fear, and you'd never do anything or go anywhere.

When you have unhealthy or paralyzing fear, it comes from a belief that you're vulnerable, that you're not safe—that, bottom line, life is random and accidental, and there's no plan, organizing force, or intelligence behind it.

Once you understand the idea that nothing is random—really understand this—you'll no longer fear other people or "bad" events. You'll no longer resent others. You'll be more willing to let other people be as they are. You'll be more willing to recognize their right to explore what they want to explore, to run their movies to conclusion—even if you don't understand and don't agree with what they're exploring.

Perhaps the idea that your director is right there with you at all times, managing everything for your benefit, can help you feel more safe, confident, and at peace.

If you have fear about death or dying, perhaps you can navigate The Invisible Path to Success and let it go by realizing that death is just the end of one total immersion movie experience.

Death does not come until you're done exploring what you want to explore, and the timing and the way it happens are not accidental. You're born when you want to start your adventure, and you die when you're done. You also choose the way your adventure ends.

Similarly, if you worry about someone close to you dying or someone close to you has died recently, consider that whether you understand their reasons or not, they wouldn't have ended their movies unless they were finished exploring what they came here to explore.

They're now off somewhere else—by choice—exploring something else. If they are or were really close to you, the odds are you've been together before and you'll be together again. You're just taking a break between films.

Chapter Thirteen

How to Follow The Invisible Path to Success in Your Relationships

Let's discuss the concept that unconscious communication is the secret force governing all relationships. To do that, I've got to divide the subject into four categories:

1. Why we have relationships in the first place.
2. How you can bring your mate, soul mate, significant other, whatever you want to call him or her, into your life. (Note: For purposes of discussion, I'll be using the word "mate.")
3. How you can bring other people into your life for companionship or to help you accomplish your goals.
4. How to make your relationships work better.

Why we have relationships in the first place

If I were to take a poll on the street this morning and ask people why they have relationships—romantic, friendship, business, whatever—I'd hear a wide variety of opinions. No matter what shape it takes, the only purpose for a relationship in Earth's amusement park is to help you explore what you came here to explore. That's it.

Remember, anyone who comes into your life and has an impact on you is there because of an ad that was placed, an ad that was responded to, or by previous agreement. That person agrees to follow your script and play a role in your movie (be it starring or supporting), and you agree to do the same for him.

There are lots of actors, actresses, and extras in "real-world" movies because they're needed if the story is going to unfold as the writer and director intend it to. It's the same with you. You need other actors, actresses, and extras to help your total immersion movie experience unfold.

No matter what it looks like on the surface in your daily life, whether others love you, support you, hurt you, betray you, or drive you crazy, they're your friends. They're doing you a great favor. They're doing exactly what you or your director asked them to do—and they're helping you do what you came here to do. Period.

It's useful to keep this in mind, especially in what might be tough times or difficult relationships.

How to bring a mate into your life

When it comes to bringing a mate into your life, the same principles we covered about how to ask and what to do if you don't receive what you asked for apply. But you must also understand that this can be a far more complicated project than many of the other projects your director manages for you.

If you want to bring a mate into your life, compose an ad and send it into the network, using your own system or following the guidelines I offered.

Then you've got to trust and flow with what you feel strongly motivated to do, understanding, once again, that what you think you want consciously or what you think would be best for you may not be what you *really* want or what would *really* be best for you.

From the time I was twenty until the time I was thirty-seven, I searched for the right woman. I spent long periods of time alone and shorter periods in relationships that didn't work or caused me a lot of pain and stress.

It was the one part of my life I could never make work. I didn't like it. I was lonely. I asked for the right woman all the time, using every technique I could find. But she never showed up. Then when I was thirty-seven, it finally happened when I met Cecily.

Cecily and I had both been going through some intense, change-filled years prior to meeting, and we're both convinced that if we'd met any earlier, or any later,

- We might not have recognized each other as the mate we were looking for.
- We might not have liked each other.
- For one reason or another, we might not have stayed together.

In fact, it's my belief that due to the unresolved emotional issues I was struggling with at the time, had we met earlier, I probably would have sabotaged the relationship or driven her away. That was a time when I wasn't a lot of fun to be with.

Yet our relationship is absolutely amazing. It's better than I could ever have imagined consciously. We met at just the right time for our relationship to blossom.

When two people decide to enter into a relationship, two movie scripts and total immersion movie experiences must be combined. Lots of details and variables must be considered and managed. Lots of changes might need to be made. It's a potentially *huge* project. Therefore, more than just about anything else you ask for, be patient when it comes to finding a mate—and remember how little you really know about what's best for you.

Ask, trust, and flow. If finding a mate is part of your movie, it'll happen when you ask. If it's not part of your movie, it won't happen when you ask.

Whenever it does happen, it'll happen with the best person for you and at the best time—no matter what you do or don't do.

How you can bring other people into your life for companionship or to help you accomplish your goals

This is one of the easiest things to do on the planet. Your director does it on your behalf all day, every day of your life. You do it without knowing you're doing it. And when you choose to become consciously involved in the process, the results can be amazing.

The process here is the same as what we've already covered. Compose an ad asking for the kind of companionship or help you need and send it into the network. Then trust and flow with what you feel strongly motivated to do.

If you've used the Internet or other online services, you've seen how easy this is to do. If you have a question or you need help with just about anything, you send a request to the right place—a Web site, a newsgroup, a special interest group, or mailing list—and people from all over the world, people you've never met and don't know and people you probably never will meet or know come out of the woodwork to help you.

It's the same with the unconscious network. Why? Because at the unconscious level we all want to help each other have the total immersion movie experiences we came here to have. Our directors are always sending ads into the network asking for what we want and responding to other people's ads offering to give what we're willing to give.

Here's another example from my life. I like doing creative work more than managing the day-to-day details of running a business. I needed to find someone who could take over those responsibilities. Here is the ad I sent into the network:

> *Please guide into my life the best person or people to help me manage my day-to-day business affairs. I want to like him or her, enjoy working with them, be able to thoroughly trust them, and know that my affairs are in good hands when I step away from daily involvement to pursue my creative projects. From the limited perspective of my conscious mind, this is what I think I want, and I ask that you give me this or something better.*

You can take a similar approach to ask for help with anything—find friendship in a new city you just moved to, find a new job, find an employee, find the best doctor to help you heal something, find a business partner, raise money to fund a project, find a mentor or coach, learn how to cook vegetarian food—anything.

No matter what you want, there's a person on the planet or a director behind the scenes who can help you create it. It's like the movie *Field of Dreams,* where the character kept hearing, "If you build it, he will come."

In this case, ask, and if it's part of your movie, it will be given to you. But please remember—only if it's part of your movie. Get as specific as is appropriate to the situation. Send the ad into the network. Then trust and flow with what you strongly feel motivated to do.

How you can make your relationships work better

Problems in relationships are caused by many things—too many to list or discuss here. But in the context of The Invisible Path to Success, problems in relationships tend to have two primary causes:

1. Mismatches in energy.
2. Programming collisions.

Mismatches in energy

Whenever you talk to someone or do something with someone, four things happen simultaneously:

1. You're both saying things, doing things, and paying attention to what happens in the *surface world*—the world of your five senses.
2. You both have thoughts about what's going on between you. I call this "inner dialogue."
3. You're both having feelings about what's going on.
4. Depending on what your movies are about, you can become consciously aware of what the other person is thinking or feeling about your interaction.

When what's said and done on the surface matches the inner dialogue and feelings beneath the surface, there may be bumps in the road, but everything generally works itself out in relationships.

If you say or do one thing on the surface (consciously), but your inner dialogue or feelings say something else at the unconscious level, and the other person becomes aware of the mismatch in energy, problems almost always result.

Why? For purposes of discussion, let's say you notice such a mismatch. The minute you notice it, a little alarm goes off in your head that says "something is wrong here" and a little wound gets ripped open because it implies there's a lack of honesty in the situation.

Then your "What does this mean?" and "How should I respond?" machine clicks into gear and tries to interpret what happened so it can choose a response. The problem is that whenever your "What does this mean?" and "How should I respond?" machine evaluates something, everything gets filtered through *your* experiences, *your* issues, *your* pain, *your* view of the world, and *your* programming. As a result, what you decide the mismatch means and what it really means can be worlds apart. Consequently, the actions you choose in response can be way off, too. That causes problems a lot of the time.

If you're very sensitive, psychic, or intuitive, your "What does this mean?" and "How should I respond?" machine might come to the correct conclusion about what the mismatch meant. But even so, damage has still been done. A wound has still been ripped open because of the dishonesty involved. As a result, problems can still occur.

This happened to me as I was growing up. I was the youngest of three children. A lot of things were said and done on the surface to suggest how loved I was, how much I was appreciated, and how much I was respected and supported, but behind the scenes, beneath the surface, the message was completely different.

At the unconscious level, there was a lot of anger and resentment about the impact my birth had on the family. There was a lot of confusion about who I really was and a lot of disapproval about how I chose to live.

Being a sensitive person, I picked up on this incredible mismatch. I heard the disapproval as clearly as if it had been spoken aloud. I felt the pain of rejection as sharply as if I'd been hit or stabbed with a knife.

I sensed the constant mismatch, struggled to interpret what it meant, and concluded it meant something was wrong with me. That started a low self-esteem cycle I struggled with for years before I discovered The Invisible Path to Success and started a new high self-esteem cycle.

In addition, because of these experiences, I concluded that what went on beneath the surface, what I sensed and felt, was real and honest and that what people said and did was unreal and dishonest. As a result, I didn't trust people for a long time. I had a hard time believing what people said to me unless it matched what I felt and was supported by a lot of proof in the form of behavior that consistently matched the words and feelings. If I sensed even the slightest mismatch in energy, my alarm bells went off and the relationship suffered in one way or another.

This is just my story, but I suspect you have your own or that you'll start noticing your own now that you've discovered this unseen force at work.

How do you stop this from happening? It's really simple: just be honest. And if you find yourself having inner dialogue or feelings that don't match what's being said or done on the surface, simply bring the inner dialogue or feelings into the open or change them internally. When you do that, not only does the mismatch disappear, but you have a great opportunity to work through some very important issues that might be impacting your relationship in a big way.

Because of my history and the damage I saw this dynamic do in the lives of people I care about, I made a decision. I decided to live by the belief that

Everything I think and feel is being heard or felt
consciously by the other people I interact with.

148

The great thing about that belief is that if I notice a mismatch in the making, I can immediately say or do something, silently or in the surface world, to resolve it before it does any damage.

Maybe you'll find living your life by the same belief to be useful too, particularly during this time of Transition, when the volume on the unconscious side of life is being turned up, our psychic and intuitive abilities are coming to life, and the potential to sense and react to energy mismatches increases daily.

Programming collisions

Programming collisions are similar to energy mismatches except the problem isn't caused by mismatches of seen and unseen forces.

Here's how a programming collision works. Someone says or does something to you. Your "What does this mean?" and "How should I respond?" machine clicks in, goes on autopilot, and attempts to interpret it.

Once again, however, your interpretation is shaped by *your* experiences, *your* issues, *your* pain, *your* view of the world, and *your* programming. As a result, what you decide others meant by what they said or did, and what they really meant by what they said or did, are often worlds apart.

Now that your unconscious machine has answered the question "What does this mean?" it moves on to answer the question "How should I respond?" Then you do something based on the meaning you chose.

Now what happens? The other person notices your response. His "What does this mean?" and "How should I respond?" machine clicks in on autopilot and he does the same thing you did: he interprets your response and chooses a response based on *his* experiences, *his* issues, *his* pain, *his* view of the world, and *his* programming.

Then you create a loop where two sets of programming are interacting on autopilot instead of two people interacting from conscious awareness and choice.

When Cecily and I have problems in our relationship, it's almost always caused by this dynamic. She says something that triggers some old pain or "neurotic pattern" in me. I react on autopilot, she reacts to my reaction, and we're off to the races. Or the same dynamic happens in reverse.

I'll give you an example. One night when we were first dating, we were supposed to meet and have dinner at her grandparents' house with a lot of people. From my perspective, I was supposed to pick Cecily up and we'd drive to her grandparents' house together. I lived an hour away up in the mountains, so I drove all the way into the city, rang her bell over and over and didn't get an answer. I was surprised. I didn't know how to get to her grandparents' house, and I didn't have their phone number. I didn't even know their last name so I could get their number from the phone book.

I'd just spent an hour driving in from the mountains and I started getting angry at what I perceived to be Cecily's carelessness and insensitivity. It pushed one of my old buttons about being taken for granted and inconvenienced. If I didn't already have this button (old programming), my reaction would not have been so strong. It was really old emotions from the past coming out, not emotions tied to the present.

Not knowing what else to do, being really mad at Cecily, and not feeling motivated to consider other, more creative, solutions to the problem, I got back in my car and drove the hour back home.

My "What does this mean?" and "How should I respond?" machine analyzed the situation, concluded

Cecily had been careless and insensitive, and chose anger as a response. Boom, boom, boom. All lightning fast, all at the unconscious level on autopilot.

That was my perspective. Now let's look at Cecily's. From Cecily's perspective, we were supposed to meet at her grandparents' house. She thought I knew how to get there because I'd been there once before. She thought she'd given me their phone number. She went over early so she could have some quiet time with her grandparents before I arrived.

When I didn't show up, she started to feel embarrassed because she was with people who were expecting to meet me, and I didn't show or even have the courtesy to call. She first thought I was being incredibly rude and inconsiderate. After a while, the embarrassment turned to worry. "Maybe he got in a car accident coming down from the mountains," she began to think.

After a while, when I still didn't show and I still didn't call, she became convinced something bad had happened to me and she got really scared.

Her "What does this mean?" and "How should I respond?" machine analyzed the situation, first concluded I was rude, then that something bad had happened to me; she chose embarrassment, then fear as her responses. Boom, boom, boom. All lightning fast, all at the unconscious level, all on autopilot.

Finally, not knowing what else to do, she called my house; having just gotten home, I answered. I was overflowing with anger and let her know it. She'd been overflowing with worry and embarrassment just as long and didn't deal very well with my anger.

To make a long story short, this is an example of what happens so often in relationships. Two "What does this mean?" and "How should I respond?" machines draw incorrect conclusions based on limited information, and problems result.

It wasn't two people interacting until we exchanged stories and cooled down; it was two sets of programming colliding.

This used to happen with me and my father when I was younger. As a result, we had a terrible relationship. But one day, we interrupted the pattern and cleared out all the old programming we had about each other. Suddenly, it was two people interacting instead of two sets of autopilot programming. We have a very good relationship today as a result.

How do you stop this dynamic from starting up or doing damage? I will offer detailed suggestions in an upcoming book and my home study course on emotions and inner experience, but here are some suggestions you can put to immediate use.

I knew I had buttons that could be pushed; I noticed when I got triggered and my autopilot responses clicked in. So I had a good starting place to ask for help. If you're like me and you know what your buttons are, send an ad into the network asking for help on the best way for you to disconnect the buttons.

If you don't know where you're being triggered into an autopilot response, send an ad into the network asking for help finding your trigger point. Or start paying attention to what's happening in your relationships when you feel bad, tense, or stressed out, or you're not getting along with someone. You'll notice patterns, and that's where the button or trigger will be found.

Once you determine what the button or trigger is, again, just send an ad into the network and ask for help to disconnect it. If it's part of your movie, you'll get the results and the relief you want. If it's not, you won't—at least not until it is what you really want.

Before we close this discussion about relationships, there are two more subjects I want to discuss. The first subject concerns judgment of other people.

Lots of problems occur in relationships because we pass judgment on who someone else is, how he acts, what he does, what his background is (or isn't), what interests him, etc., and we act accordingly.

When you look at someone else, or someone else's life, you see it through your own filters—through your own "What does this mean?" and "How should I respond?" machine.

As a result, and as we've discussed many times in this book, what you see may or may not be what's really there. This, in and of itself, is enough reason to resist judging another human being, for how can you judge when you don't even know if you're clearly seeing what's there?

But it goes deeper than that. If you look at it from the perspective of The Invisible Path to Success, you have absolutely no conscious idea what someone else's movie is about or what the goal of a particular scene is.

You don't know what inner experiences he's having, what interests him at the deepest level, or what he came here to explore. You don't know where his movie is headed or where it will end up.

Again I ask, how can we possibly feel justified in judging anyone or anything? We see and know so little about ourselves, much less the other people we see or interact with.

Adopting a nonjudgmental attitude can dramatically reduce your stress and improve your relationships and self-esteem. It can also improve the self-esteem of others.

We're all interested in different things. If that weren't the case, there would be no libraries, no radio and movie archives, no Internet, no online special interest groups, no Web pages, and no cable or satellite television with hundreds of channels on every conceivable subject.

Look around the world. Billions of people are exploring different realities. Perhaps, unless it's part of our movies to do otherwise, we can all learn to let each other explore in peace.

The final point I want to make about relationships is this:

Everyone who's in your life right now,
everyone who has ever been in your life and
everyone who will ever be in your life
in the future is your very best friend.

They were willing to take time away from their explorations to invest time, energy, and effort into helping you with your total immersion movie. No matter what kind of impact they're having on your life or what you think about them, they're doing you a huge favor.

They wouldn't be there if you hadn't asked them to be there. They wouldn't be doing what they're doing unless you asked them to do it. And you wouldn't have asked them to do it unless there was some benefit you could receive from it—even if you can't see the benefit now or you never consciously see it!

Perhaps you'll find it useful to feel some gratitude from time to time (even if the person has hurt you, is hurting you now, or drives you absolutely crazy most of the time).

Chapter Fourteen

**How to Navigate The Invisible Path to
Success in Your Career, Business, and Finances**

If you're in sales, marketing, or business of any kind, remember the potential problems that energy mismatches can represent. Make sure your outer words and actions match your inner dialogue and feelings, or there could be problems with your clients, customers, employees, or bosses.

Remember, in the surface world you can limit what you share about who you really are. But in the unconscious world, you're an open book. There are no secrets behind the scenes.

I started a business several years ago that did very well for its first eight months then fell apart suddenly and for no apparent "earthbound" reason. In evaluating what happened and why, I discovered some mismatches between what was written in our marketing materials, what was actually offered in the product we were selling, and what was going on *inside* the employees of the company.

I also discovered some damaging P.S.'s that had been added to the ads we were sending into the network asking for success with the project. Because of the mismatches and the P.S.'s, we attracted a different kind of customer than we wanted, we had a lot of problems, and we ultimately went out of business after losing a lot of money. Had the mismatches been resolved and the P.S.'s uncovered and changed, the business would have been successful.

Suppose two people open separate businesses to sell the same product. Suppose they both approach you and ask you to buy it. Suppose, regardless of what they say or do on the surface, the unconscious ad of one of them says:

> *I've got a good product. It might help you. It might not. But I want you to buy it anyway. If it doesn't work for you, I'll give you your money back.*

But suppose there's also a P.S. in the ad that says:

> *By the way, I really want you to buy it because I need the money to make my car payment. And I hope you don't ask for your money back, because I'll have trouble giving it to you.*

Suppose the other person's unconscious ad says:

> *I have a great product. I've been working with it for ten years, and I'm confident it can help you. I'd like you to buy it and if it doesn't work for you, just return it and I'll give you your money back. I don't want your money unless I know I've helped you solve your problem.*

If both people were offering the same product at the same price with the same guarantee, which one would you want to buy it from: the first one or the second one? The second one, right? It delivers a more appealing and welcoming message.

This might seem like a silly example, but from the perspective of The Invisible Path to Success, it happens in business all the time without us knowing about it. As individuals and companies, we spend a lot of time, money, and energy trying to control or manipulate what goes on at the surface level.

More often than not, what's going on at the unconscious level and what we're sending through the unconscious network determine whether our businesses or careers succeed or fail—not the surface activity we're so concerned with.

It might be part of your movie to explore what happens when there are energy mismatches in business. That was the case for me at one point in my life. But in case it isn't what you want to explore, my suggestion to you is to make sure you resolve your energy mismatches in business by being totally honest up-front, and defusing any others you might notice, by bringing them out into the open (in one way or another).

If you want a new job, more sales, a healthier business, or whatever, by all means, do what you feel motivated to do in the surface world. But remember to follow the guidelines already suggested and to send ads into the unconscious network asking for help with it.

When you tap into the unconscious network, the people who want what you have to offer will always find their way to you—if it's a good match. Their directors will see to it.

In many ways, I've come to believe that the things we do at the conscious level only create doorways for people who find out about us at the unconscious level to walk through and connect with us.

Let me give you an example. My sister, Shaina Noll, has built up a very successful music business she runs out of her home selling two CD titles she recorded. The most famous of her titles is "Songs for the Inner Child." She's done very little advertising, marketing, or "surface activity," yet she does quite well and has a wonderful lifestyle with her family. Why? Because through the unconscious network, the people who could benefit from her music find out about her, then find their way to buying her music. And because part of her movie is about exploring what can be done to grow a business without a lot of surface activity.

It's the same thing for this book and the home study course with the same name. I did things to promote the book and course that traditional wisdom said wouldn't work. But everything I did on the surface had an unconscious ad, an unconscious message from my director attached to it. Other directors read the ad, got the message, and saw to it that the right people responded to the surface activity—even though the odds were against it.

The same thing is happening with you right now, and if you start participating in the process a little more consciously, I think you'll be pleasantly surprised by the results you'll produce.

Our culture, books, and movies; the media; and many of our parents, mentors, and role models tell us that success—for everyone—means having a lot of money and a fancy lifestyle. Consequently, many of us, maybe you too, feel a lot of pressure to be financially successful.

As I've come to see it, having a lot of money, having the amount of money you consciously ask for, or having the money you want within the time frame you want it may not be what your movie is about. It may not be what you came here to explore—regardless of what you were taught, what you were programmed to believe at the surface level, what other people around you are exploring or experiencing, or what you consciously think is best for you.

I grew up in a family that had a very neurotic relationship with money. I was programmed and pressured to continue the same neurotic patterns, and they caused me a lot of stress, frustration, and pain.

I've had times in my life when I had no money and times in my life when I had a lot of money. In each case, as I see so clearly now, the amount I had was perfect for what my movie was about at the time and for what I really needed to complete a set of specific and very important scenes. In each case, the presence or lack of money set certain things in motion in my inner experience that helped me move to where I am now, which I'm extremely pleased about.

I now recognize the wisdom of my director, even though I didn't at the time. Through the experiences I had, and the money phases I went through, I released a lot of old "neurotic patterns" about money, and now—finally at age forty—I have a healthy relationship with it.

You will have only as much money as it takes (or as much as is allowed) to make sure you have the total immersion movie experience you came here for. No more, no less. It doesn't matter what you believe, what you do, how hard you try, or who you learn about money-making from. That's just the way it is.

Remember, you always get a vote, but you don't always win the election!

One last thing. Right now, consciously, you may have no idea about what the role of money is in your movie. You may have no idea how much money is part of your movie or how much is allowed as part of what you came to explore.

So if you want more money in your life or you want to change your relationship with money, follow the guidelines I've shared here (or your own variation of them). Send an ad into the network asking to be guided to the people, ideas, resources, opportunities, and actions that can help you do it, then trust and flow with what you feel *strongly* motivated to do as a result.

You may just receive what you ask for—or something even better!

Closing Remarks

We've now taken seven very big and important steps together. Here they are again as a brief review:

1. Let go of opinions and use what works *for you.*
2. Take your seats to the best show in town.
3. Turn off the cruise control.
4. Reach out and touch someone.
5. Tap *all* your resources.
6. You always get a vote, but you don't always win the election.
7. Sail with the winds of change.

The poet T.S. Eliot once wrote:

> *We shall not cease from exploration; and the end of all our explorations will be to arrive where we started, only to know the place for the first time.*

We started this book by asking the question, What is success? Following Mr. Eliot's lead, let us return to where we started by asking the same question again—this time able to fully answer it for the first time.

What is success? Success, in general, is simply doing what you came here to do. Success is having the total immersion movie experience you came here to have. Nothing more, nothing less.

Do you know what's so interesting about that? You're already doing it! You're already there. You're already incredibly successful—no matter what you think consciously.

Due to the way our total immersion movies are set up in the first place, and the involvement of your director as each scene is filmed and your script comes to life, success in your movie over the course of your lifetime is absolutely guaranteed!

If you've been feeling like a failure, like your life hasn't amounted to anything, or like you have no direction, know that you are a total success, no matter what happened in the previous scenes or what's happening in the current scene.

When your movie is over and you choose to leave this amusement park, you'll have experienced everything you wanted to experience when you decided to come here—every last ounce of thought, feeling, and learning you wanted.

When it's all said and done, all that matters is the inner experiences imprinted on your memory records and those inner experiences you imprint or help imprint on the memory records of others.

When you walk out of a movie theater after a really good movie, what are you left with? What you've experienced inside yourself. That's all there is. You leave the rest in the theater and it all fades in importance.

So give yourself a break! Be gentle with yourself. Relax a bit. And always remember, while you may not consciously know what success in your movie should look or feel like, your director does know and he will get you there, no matter what it takes.

"Well Bob," you might be thinking, "if I'm already so successful and I'm going to get what I came for, what's the point of this book?"

I have two answers for you. First, perhaps you wanted this book to help you consciously see that you are already successful. Second, when movies are filmed, the director, cast, and crew tap lots of resources to make it all happen. Perhaps there are resources in this book you or your director wanted to tap—consciously—to help you film your scenes or complete your movie.

Success in general is to do what you came here to do, but success at this particular point has a slight twist to it.

To be successful during the Transition means becoming consciously aware of who you really are and what you really want, then consciously bringing all of your life—your career, relationships, lifestyle, everything—into alignment with the real you and your real purpose.

That process will look completely different for you than it will for me and everyone else, but that is what success means during this special time in history. It's a very important part of your movie and the reason behind why you chose to film it now.

This book is called *The Invisible Path to Success* because so much of what creates your daily life, what shapes your thoughts and feelings, and what happens to you is invisible—behind the scenes.

That's the way it was meant to be—at least for now. But we can still map out enough streets, roads, and highways on The Invisible Path to Success to navigate where we *really* want to go.

You may or may not agree with everything I've said here. You may or may not use the suggestions or guidelines I offered you. But if I succeeded in stimulating you, opening your mind, or getting you to consider another path to your chosen destination, I'll feel I've done my job well.

If anything I've shared here helps you feel less fear in your life, helps you be gentler with yourself, helps you forgive yourself and others a bit, or helps you feel more safe, protected, and guided during the seemingly crazy times we live in, I'll also feel I've done my job.

There's so much pressure on us to be someone other than who we really are. If you receive nothing else from this book, I hope you'll feel a renewed sense of permission to be who you really are, do what you really want to do, and follow your heart and dreams—even if there's resistance from other people around you.

Remember, we're all equals down here. We all come here with the same amount of power, the same potential, the same raw ability. We just choose to focus it differently, explore different things, and develop different skills.

If something interests you, that's enough reason to do it and is significant in and of itself. What you explore does not need to contribute to society, give a lot to others, be grand or dramatic, be societally acceptable, or earn you fame or fortune.

All your life needs to do is give you the inner experiences you want to have. That's it.

I'm very interested in knowing how this book has impacted you. I know you're busy and it's a lot to ask, but I'd love it if you'd write or e-mail me to let me know how you're doing, ask any questions you might have, or tell me about your success stories.

You can also contact me to get on my mailing list or to find out about other tools that can make your navigation of The Invisible Path to Success as precise as possible.

You can reach me as follows:

By Mail: Invisible Path Publishing
20505 U.S. 19 North, Ste. 12-338
Clearwater, FL 33764

Online: bob@invisiblepath.com
http://www.invisiblepath.com

A famous poem called *Desiderata* has the tone, energy, and feeling I'd like to leave you with as you begin your personal navigation of The Invisible Path to Success.

Desiderata

Go quietly amid the noise and haste and remember what peace there may be in silence. As far as possible without surrender, be on good terms with all persons. Speak your truth quietly and clearly; and listen to others, even to the dull and ignorant; they too have their story.

Avoid loud and aggressive persons; they are vexatious to the spirit. If you compare yourself with others you may become bitter or vain, for there will always be greater and lesser persons than yourself. Enjoy your achievements as well as your plans.

Keep interested in your own career, however humble; it is a real possession in the changing fortunes of our time. Exercise caution in your business affairs, for the world is full of trickery; but let this not blind you to what virtue there is.

Be yourself. Especially do not feign affection. Neither be cynical about love, for in the face of aridity and disenchantment, it is as perennial as the grass.

Take kindly the counsel of years, gracefully surrendering the things of youth. Nurture strength of spirit to shield you in sudden misfortune, but do not distress yourself with dark imaginings.

Many fears are born of fatigue and loneliness. Beyond a wholesome discipline be gentle with yourself. You are a child of the universe no less than the trees and the stars; you have a right to be here, and whether or not it is clear to you, no doubt the universe is unfolding as it should.

Therefore, be at peace with God, whatever you conceive Him to be. And whatever your labours and aspirations, in the noisy confusion of life, keep peace in your soul. With all its sham, drudgery, and broken dreams, it is still a beautiful world. Be cheerful. Strive to be happy.

(Note: This anonymous poem was found in old Saint Paul's Church in Baltimore, Maryland.)

Here are my final words to you. Remember who you really are and why you're really here. Remember that the whole game is about inner experiences and exploring what you want to explore.

Be gentle with yourself. Give yourself a break. Forgive yourself for any imagined mistakes, errors, or failures. They were all part of your movie script.

You need never again use "generic" or "hit or miss" strategies for getting what you really want in life. Decide what you think you want. Send ads into the network asking for your own customized solutions and answers. Trust that you'll get what you asked for—or something even better. Flow with what you feel *strongly* motivated to do.

Remember that the director part of you is always there at your side, twenty-four hours a day, seven days a week. He or she is helping you, protecting you, working overtime to make sure you get everything you came here to experience. You're never alone and you can't make a mistake.

Pleasant journeys and I'll see you at the movies!

Hampton Roads Publishing Company

. . .for the evolving human spirit

Hampton Roads Publishing Company
publishes and distributes books on a variety of subjects,
including metaphysics, health, complementary medicine,
visionary fiction, and other related topics.

To order or receive a copy of our latest catalog,
call toll-free, (800) 766-8009,
or send your name and address to:

Hampton Roads Publishing Company, Inc.
134 Burgess Lane
Charlottesville, VA 22902

Internet: www.hrpub.com
e-mail: hrpc@hrpub.com